Better Homes and Gardens.

carpentry
& trimwork

Step-by-Step

TABLE OF CONTENTS

Ideas
TO BUILD YOUR DREAMS   10

Carpentry
PROJECTS   16

Tools
AND MATERIALS 80

Carpentry
TECHNIQUES 104

INTRODUCTION

Many people think that only professionals with years of experience can handle carpentry projects. As a result, they pay large amounts of money to contractors without knowing if they are getting a fair price or quality workmanship. Others believe that anyone can do carpentry projects. They plunge unprepared into jobs they are not able to handle. The results often are disastrous. A person with little or no experience will not be able to cut a straight line, much less construct a wall or build a cabinet. Basic carpentry skills are within reach of any homeowner, but they require instruction and practice. If you take the time to learn the basics, you will be able to succeed at a variety of carpentry jobs.

Step-by-Step Carpentry explains how wood structures are put together and what you need to know to tackle home repairs and improvements. This book will show you, one step at a time, how to fix minor and major problems and how to build new walls, ceilings, and floors. Many other smaller projects—such as installing molding, planning for and installing new cabinets, building decorative molding shelves, and organizing a bedroom closet—also are included. Projects such as these enable you to add decorative touches to your house and maximize the existing spaces. You'll also find many common repair projects included in the book. You don't need to resign yourself to living with a door that squeaks or sticks, and you can install a deadbolt lock to help keep your family secure.

Once you have learned basic carpentry techniques, you can save money by doing projects yourself— and you'll experience the satisfaction of completing well-built structures with your own hands. Even when you choose to pay someone to do work

you feel is beyond your skill level, you'll be able to make sure that the job has been done correctly and at a fair price.

How to use this book
Begin by reading "Safety" and "Working to Code" on pages 6–7. Though you'll see "Caution" boxes throughout the book that will help you remain safe as you complete a particular project, it's important to be familiar with overall safety procedures to ensure you work safely from the very beginning of every project. In addition, "Working to Code" tells you when you'll be required to obtain a permit before beginning a project or when you'll need to meet building code specifications. It's critical that you obtain these before beginning a project so that your plans can be approved and so that you'll know at what stages the project will need to be inspected. "Getting to Know Your Home" on pages 8–9 will help you understand specific parts of your home's structure and how a house is built.

The section "Carpentry Projects" discusses specific projects; you can read and study all of these now or wait until you plan to undertake one of them to read about it. This section will introduce you to a variety of projects from basic ones such as building a work area to more complex ones such as installing kitchen countertops and cabinets. Look through this section for ideas and inspiration for projects that will enhance your home. Each project contains a "You'll Need" box that details approximately how long a project will take, what skills are required to complete the project, and what tools are necessary. If you don't have the tools necessary to complete a job, turn to the "Tools and Materials" chapter for information

that will help when you buy or rent the tools you need. This section also will help acquaint you with the lumber and hardware that is available to you. You will learn which tools are the best and how to select the best materials for your project.

If you want to learn new carpentry skills or brush up on current ones, read the final section, "Carpentry Techniques," to get an idea of the basic procedures involved in most carpentry projects. This chapter describes the proper usage and care of the tools you'll use and the techniques involved in using them. It's always a good idea to practice seldom-used skills and techniques before beginning the actual project.

Tip boxes
In addition to the basic instructions and "You'll Need" information boxes, you'll find plenty of additional tips throughout the book. Pay special attention to the "Caution" boxes. When a how-to step requires special care, "Caution" warns you what to watch out for. It will help keep you from doing damage to yourself or the job at hand.

Other information boxes provide helpful hints such as how to take accurate measurements using special measuring techniques and how to cut costs with tips on accurately estimating your material needs, making wise tool purchases, and organizing the job to minimize wasted labor. Other information boxes provide tricks of the trade that experts have learned over a lifetime of professional carpentry work. These tips can make all the difference in helping you do a job quickly and well with information on methods and materials that make a job easier.

CARPENTRY CAN BE FUN

Carpentry projects can be rewarding both for the end result and the craftsmanship involved in the process. To learn how to complete projects, turn to "Carpentry Projects," page 16. For information about the skills involved in carpentry, turn to page 104, "Carpentry Techniques."

SAFETY

Tool safety tips

Safety is the result of following guidelines and exercising common sense. You can hurt yourself with hand tools; when working with a power tool, just one moment's lapse of concentration can lead to serious injury. To minimize risks, keep the following guidelines in mind:

■ Use tools only for the jobs they were designed to do. If a tool came with an instruction manual, take the time to read it to find out what the tool will do and what it will not do.

■ Check on the condition of a tool before using it. A dull cutting edge or a loose-fitting hammerhead, for example, spells trouble. Also inspect the cord of a power tool to make sure it's not damaged.

■ Don't work with tools if you're tired or in a hurry.

■ Don't work with tools if you have recently been drinking alcohol.

■ Wear goggles whenever the operation you are performing could result in eye injury.

■ The safety mechanisms on power tools are there for your protection.

Don't tamper with or remove them from the tool.

■ Don't wear loose-fitting clothes or dangling jewelry while you are using tools.

■ Keep other people, especially children, at a safe distance while you're using any tool. Before you let children use a tool, instruct them on how to operate it and supervise them as they work.

■ Before servicing or adjusting a power tool, unplug it and allow moving parts to stop.

> **PROTECT YOURSELF**

Safety equipment is a must for any project. Always wear safety goggles. Even if you wear glasses, safety glasses are important because they provide a greater area of coverage than standard lenses. Wear a dust mask or a respirator when cutting and sanding and when undertaking demolition work. Many carpentry power tools are extremely loud—use earplugs or hearing protectors when operating them. Wear a cap to keep dust and debris out of your hair, and put on a hardhat for demolition work.

WORKING TO CODE

Although you may be an amateur working on your own house, you have the same responsibilities to building authorities as a professional carpenter or contractor. Any structure you build must be solid and long-lasting, plumb and square, and constructed of materials appropriate for the job. That means using only those techniques and materials that meet your local building codes.

The procedures in this book will satisfy most local codes, but be aware that codes can vary widely. Always check with your city or county building department if you are considering adding to or changing the structure of your house in any substantial way or if you believe your existing structures might be substandard.

Building codes may seem bothersome, but they are designed to make your home safe and worry-free. Ignoring codes can lead to costly mistakes, health hazards, and even difficulties in someday selling your house. Minor repairs do not require permits. However, changes involving framing; major projects, such as kitchen or bath remodeling or adding a new room; or jobs affecting plumbing and electrical systems typically require permits. If you are in doubt, check with your building department before proceeding. Neglecting to do so could cause you the expense and trouble of tearing out and redoing work. (In the course of completing carpentry work, you will expose wiring and pipes. Take a little time to make sure these systems are safe and up to code before you cover them up again.)

There's no telling what kind of building inspector you will encounter when you apply for your permit or when they inspect your site: Some can be helpful, friendly, and flexible; others are rigid and unyielding, focusing on every small detail. No matter what kind of inspector you deal with, your work will go better if you follow these guidelines:

■ To avoid unnecessary questions about your plans, seek out as much information as possible and incorporate that information into your plan before you take it in for approval. Your building department may have literature explaining requirements for the type of project you have planned.

■ Go to your building department with a plan to be approved or amended; don't expect the inspectors to plan the job for you. Present your plan with neatly drawn diagrams and a complete list of the materials you will be using.

■ Be sure you understand clearly at what stages of your project you need to have inspections. Do not cover up plumbing or electrical installations that need to be inspected by finishing the walls or floors before the inspector gets there, for instance.

■ Be as courteous as possible. Take time to do high-quality work. Inspectors often are wary of homeowners because so many do shoddy work. Show the inspector you are serious about doing things the correct way.

CHECK CODES BEFORE YOU BEGIN
A complete kitchen remodeling project such as this one requires checking with your local building department for necessary permits before you begin the project. Doing so will ultimately save you time and effort.

When you plan a carpentry project or go to a building supply center for materials, it helps to know the common terms describing the parts of your house. Some of these terms vary from region to region, but most are understood throughout the country. Although this book deals primarily with interior carpentry projects, it is useful to be able to visualize how your house is put together. Even a task as simple as attaching a wall shelf or installing baseboard molding requires some knowledge of framing.

The house shown *at right* combines the elements of old and new construction—a situation you may find in your own home. The two-story section of the house shows construction methods and materials common between 1910 and 1960. The one-story addition shows materials and techniques in common use by contractors today.

Framing is the skeleton of your house, the basic structure holding it together. Vertical **wall studs** run from floor to ceiling. They're usually made of 2×4s, but sometimes 2×6s or even 2×8s are used to allow space for more insulation. The horizontal pieces at the top and bottom of the walls are called **plates.** The bottom plate rests on a **concrete block** or **formed concrete foundation.** Walls may have **fire blocking** running horizontally about halfway up the wall.

Wherever there is an opening for a door or a window, a correctly sized **header,** made of a single piece of lumber or two pieces of 2× lumber, must span the gap in the framing. For more details about framing, see pages 51–54 and 68–69.

Roofs are supported by either **rafters** or **trusses,** which use small-dimensioned lumber joined in such a way as to give them strength. **Collar ties** brace the rafters. The roof typically is made of **plywood** or boards covered with **roofing felt** and **shingles. Eaves** are trimmed with **fascia boards. Vents** draw hot air from the attic.

Joists made of 2×6 to 2×12 lumber support **subfloors, flooring,** and interior load-bearing walls. The undersides of joists provide nailing surfaces for ceilings.

On the exterior walls, the framing is covered with at least three layers of material. First comes **sheathing,** which in older homes is made of 1× lumber run diagonally. When it's milled with an overlapping joint, it is called **shiplap.** Plywood, oriented-strand board (OSB), fiberboard, or rigid foam is used in newer homes. Next comes a paperlike layer to improve insulation and reduce the effects of condensation. Older homes use **roofing felt** (also called tar paper) or reddish-colored building paper; newer homes have **house wrap,** often made of polyethylene. Finally, the house is clad in siding. This house has horizontal **beveled siding,** but vertical siding and sheet siding also are common. Inside the exterior walls, older homes often have gray-colored **rock wool (asbestos) insulation; fiberglass** is used now.

Interior wall surfaces of older homes usually are covered with **lath,** thin pieces of rough, ⅜-inch thick wood, run horizontally. The lath is covered with two or three layers of **plaster.** Today **drywall** is nailed or screwed to the framing, and the joints and nail holes are covered with joint compound. Plastering is a specialized skill that takes years to learn, but a homeowner can apply and finish drywall (see pages 74–77).

Gaps around windows (**double-hung sash, casement, fixed-pane,** or **full-round),** doors and along walls are covered with molding. See pages 20–26 for installing moldings.

Vent

Full-round window

Fixed-pane window

Beveled siding

Hardwood flooring

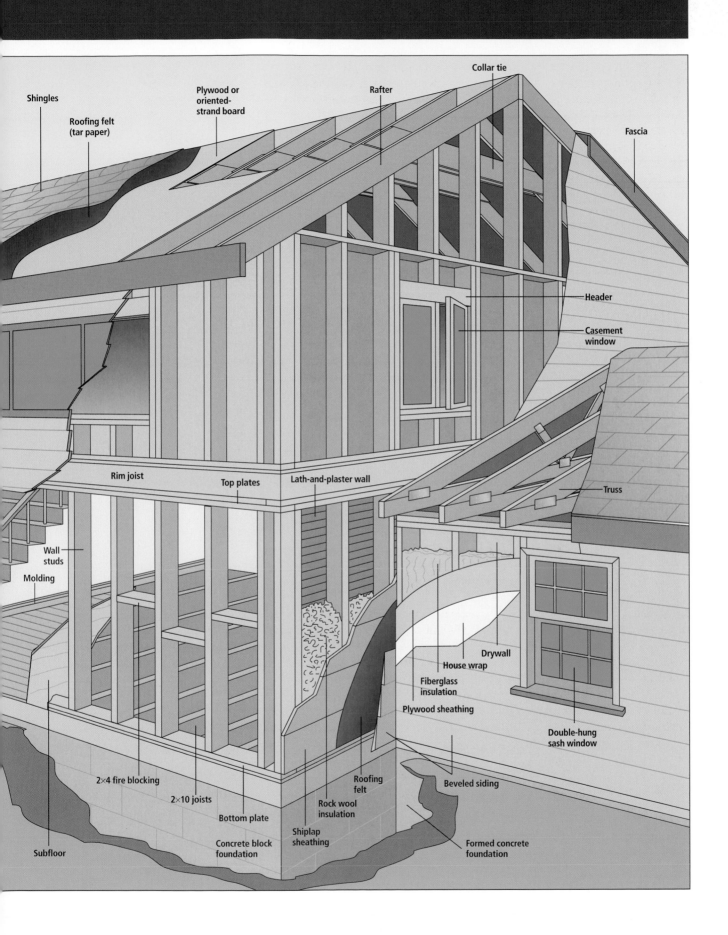

Shingles

Roofing felt
(tar paper)

Plywood or
oriented-
strand board

Rafter

Collar tie

Fascia

Header

Casement
window

Rim joist

Top plates

Lath-and-plaster wall

Truss

Wall
studs

Molding

Drywall

House wrap

Fiberglass
insulation

Plywood sheathing

Double-hung
sash window

2×4 fire blocking

2×10 joists

Bottom plate

Roofing
felt

Rock wool
insulation

Beveled siding

Subfloor

Concrete block
foundation

Shiplap
sheathing

Formed concrete
foundation

Ideas
TO BUILD YOUR DREAMS

Y ou can realize your remodeling dreams through carpentry. This book demystifies the

basics of carpentry. You will discover the techniques and cultivate the basic skills you need

to organize that closet, build a bookcase, and remodel your kitchen. Upgrade your home with

simple facelifts. Rework your floor plan to create new, functional space. Finish an existing

basement. Create elegance with trim molding. Add spice with decorative shelves. The

following pages present ideas to jump-start your imagination. To transform your remodeling

ideas into reality, you'll find both easy and more advanced step-by-step projects in this book.

CREATE A BONUS ROOM
Laying out and cutting drywall may not be your dream project, but it can lead to a bonus family room with space for a pool table, bar, and conversation area. After furring basement walls or building a new wall (see pages 51–54 and 68–71), follow the drywall project steps beginning on page 72. Then get ready to finalize the details for your bonus space.

CREATE A FOCAL POINT
Wall-mounted plate rails turn a previously blank wall into a decorative focal point in a breakfast room. Turn to page 42 for how to build decorative molding shelves and pages 60–63 for planning for and installing chair rails.

REPLICATE A BUILT-IN
This shelf unit—deep enough to display a collection of plates—combines windowsill, casing, and other stock moldings. The chair rail serves as the base for the plate rack. See page 63 to build a custom chair rail and page 42 to build decorative shelves with molding.

WHITEN AND BRIGHTEN

Install all-white cabinetry to brighten a kitchen. Before purchasing cabinets, consider what storage needs you have and choose cabinet features accordingly. Base cabinets, for example, are available with pullout shelves that make it easy to reach items at the back.

CREATE A TRANSITION

This room breaks the tradition of a thick band of crown molding. Instead a stylish thin band of crown molding creates a polished transition between the walls and ceiling. Page 20 shows molding ideas.

ADD A HOME OFFICE
Expand the living space in your home by creating a den or home office in a previously unfinished basement. Turn to pages 51–54 to build walls. See page 70 for furring basement walls. Drywalling projects begin on Page 72.

EXPAND FAMILY SPACE
Once a new wall was built to enclose this basement poolroom, the space was finished. The ceiling joists, wires, and pipes were left exposed and painted brown. The open ceiling gives more headroom than a finished ceiling and simplifies the project. See pages 51–54 to build a new wall.

INSTALL DECORATIVE TOUCHES

Finish off a room with stylish details such as crown molding and trim molding around windows. Turn to page 21 to learn how to install molding.

Turn to page 21 to learn how to install molding.

REMODEL A DATED KITCHEN

Cut the cost of remodeling a kitchen by installing the cabinets yourself. Turn to page 27 to plan for new cabinet installation. When you're ready to install, see page 29 for base cabinets and page 31 for wall cabinets.

Turn to page 27 to plan for new cabinet installation. When you're ready to install, see page 29 for base cabinets and page 31 for wall cabinets.

Carpentry
PROJECTS

Most projects in this book share the same preparation techniques. This chapter details the steps necessary to complete construction. Read the steps and suggestions carefully before you begin to make sure you understand what is required. If you're unsure of your skills, consider hiring a professional to complete difficult steps.

Lay out your project and organize it into stages. Breaking a large project into small stages allows you to work efficiently. Large projects such as kitchen remodeling will make the space unusable for a long period of time. Thorough project planning is essential.

Create a shopping list. Include materials as well as tools. Check off those you already have and purchase those you need. It is better to purchase extra of some materials such as screws and nails, rather than running back and forth to the store each time you run out of them.

Consult with your local building inspector to determine if you'll need a permit. If a permit is required, begin the work after the inspector has approved your plans.

CREATE KITCHEN CHARACTER

This chapter includes all of the carpentry projects involved in remodeling a kitchen such as this one. Kitchen projects often begin with installing new base and wall cabinets. New laminate countertops provide an improved work surface. Installing new windows can afford greater comfort and energy efficiency. Top off the project with shelves to hold collectibles and kitchen necessities.

INSTALL DISPLAY SPACE

Ceiling-hung cabinets are a great solution to provide additional storage or display space above an island. Turn to page 33 to install ceiling-hung cabinets.

QUIET A SQUEAKY DOOR

As homes subtly settle and shift, fixing door problems becomes one of the most common—and simple—carpentry projects. To keep doors opening smoothly and quietly, see the suggestions on page 44.

BUILDING A WORKBENCH

Strength and durability define a well-built workbench. The heavy-duty legs of this workbench provide the strength to support large projects. The double-layered top withstands the blows of pounding. When the top layer becomes damaged from use, the design allows you to remove and replace it with a new hardboard surface.

Load up the bottom shelf with tools and materials—the extra weight will make the bench more stable. The perforated hardboard back provides handy tool storage. If you want to skip the tool board just cut the back legs to the same length as the front.

PRECUTS

Quantity	Piece	Length
2	2×4 rear legs	69⅝"
2	2×4 front legs	32"
4	2×4 short legs	28½"
4	2×4 rails	54"
4	2×4 side braces	25⅜"
1	2×6 front brace	57"
1	½" plywood shelf	19½"×57"
2	¾" plywood top	23⅞"×60"
1	¼" perforated hardboard	36"×54"
2	1×3 tool board frame sides	36"
1	1×3 tool board frame top	55½"
2	1×3 tool board rails	54"

YOU'LL NEED

TIME: About 4 hours.

SKILLS: Precise measuring and cutting, gluing, nailing, driving screws.

TOOLS: Tape measure, circular saw or tablesaw, drill and driver bit, hammer, nail set.

1 ASSEMBLE THE LEGS.

Assemble the short legs to the front legs and to the rear legs using glue and 2½-inch drywall screws. Use a drill with the proper-size Phillips-head driver bit to make short work of the assembly.

2 ATTACH HORIZONTAL PIECES.

Screw the top rails into the leg notches, flush to the outside of the legs. To locate the bottom of the lower rails and the side braces, lay out lines 6 inches from the bottom of the legs. Screw the rails to the inside of the legs, and then screw the side pieces to the outside of the legs.

3 ATTACH THE LOWER SHELF.

Place the lower shelf on top of the lower rails and side braces. Secure it with 1¼-inch drywall screws.

4 CONSTRUCT THE TOP.

Put the first layer of plywood in place against the back leg extensions and centered side to side. Fasten it to the frame with 1¼-inch drywall screws. Screw the second plywood piece in place with 3-inch drywall screws driven through both layers of plywood into the bench.

5 FINISH THE SURFACE.

Place the ⅛-inch hardboard on top of the plywood top, flush on all sides. Drive 4d finishing nails through the work surface to the plywood. Drive the nails slightly below the surface using a nail set.

6 INSTALL THE TOOL PANEL.

Place the perforated hardboard against the leg extensions with its bottom edge resting on the bench surface. Attach the perforated hardboard to the leg extensions with ¾-inch drywall screws.

7 ASSEMBLE THE TOOL PANEL FRAME.

Use ¾-inch drywall screws to attach the panel side frame pieces to the leg extensions. Attach the rails to the leg extensions with 2-inch drywall screws. Drive ¾-inch screws through the back of the perforated hardboard into the rails. Use 1½-inch screws to attach the top board to the leg extensions and top rail.

MOLDING IDEAS

Dress up a room without using paint or wallpaper. Change just one subtle detail and make a statement. Trim adds a distinctive touch. Base molding frames walls. Crown molding adds elegance; it provides an architectural detail that gives character to a room. Trim molding can be a simple strip of wood or an elaborate creation incorporating different elements of designs, materials, and finishes. The following pages will help you transform dull, ordinary spaces into elegant rooms. You'll see examples of trimwork that will help you come up with ideas for your space then learn the basics of how to install base trim and crown molding.

ADD VISUAL INTEREST TO WALLS

To add drama to walls, apply crown molding where the walls meet the ceiling and chair rail molding slightly below the crown molding. In this living room, the walls are painted one rich hue and the space between moldings another to highlight the stylish wall treatment.

AVOID CUTTING CORNERS

Lightweight materials such as urethane foam make installing ornate crown moldings a snap. Some of these moldings even come with preformed corners that eliminate the effort of precisely mitering the corners. If the look you want is not available in a foam molding, combine pieces to create a custom look.

INSTALLING BASE MOLDING

Base molding runs along the bottom of the wall at the floor. Base moldings vary from simple square-edge boards to profiled moldings. Baseboards often are finished with a base shoe, a molding much like a quarter round that fits at the bottom of the base molding against the floor. When the wall is longer than available moldings, join two pieces with a butt splice in an inconspicuous location. Where the joint will show, use a scarf joint for a more professional look.

Base molding basics

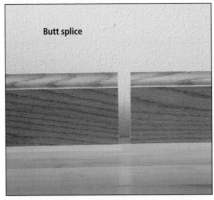

Butt splice

Install the corner piece first, then the baseboards.

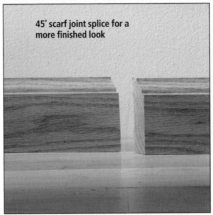

45° scarf joint splice for a more finished look

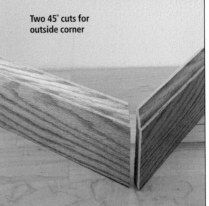

Two 45° cuts for outside corner

BUYING MOLDING

Molding can be expensive, so determine exactly how many pieces of each size you need. On a piece of paper, make columns for each size—8 feet, 10 feet, 12 feet, etc. As you measure for individual pieces, tally how many you need under each column. If you have an old house, you may need moldings that are no longer made. A millwork company can probably make replicas. If the price is too high or you need only a small piece of molding, you may be able to make a reasonable facsimile using a router, tablesaw, radial-arm saw, and belt sander.

YOU'LL NEED

TIME: About 10 minutes per piece of molding.

SKILLS: Precise measuring and cutting, figuring out the direction of cuts, nailing.

TOOLS: Tape measure, try square, miter box and backsaw or power mitersaw, coping saw, rasp, block plane, hammer, nail set.

MEASURE AND MARK PRECISELY.

Whenever possible, hold a piece of molding in place and mark it with a knife or sharp pencil, rather than using a tape measure.

1 START ON A SHORT WALL.

If you have a piece of molding that is longer than the wall, you can install the base with just one strip. Cut each end at 90 degrees to run directly into each corner. Measure for the length of the next piece. If the wall is longer than the trim, you will need to make a scarf joint splice. Try to place the cut so that it will be over a stud.

Installing base molding *(continued)*

Installing molding to finish off a project can be the most gratifying part of the job. Although it's easier than you might expect, it takes some practice. Start installing molding where it will be the least visible. You'll soon surprise yourself with your speed and neat joinery. The most common mistake is to cut a miter in the wrong direction. Whenever possible, mark pieces clearly, not only for length but also for the direction of the cut.

Install door and window casing and other vertical molding before you install molding at the bottom of your walls. Choose from ranch or colonial base molding or use a three-piece base for a traditional look. It is best to add a quarter round or base shoe as well. These types bend easily with variations in the flooring and buffer molding from vacuum cleaner scuffs.

You may be tempted simply to miter-cut pieces for inside corners. This often leads to unsightly gaps and misaligned joints because the corners are almost never true 90-degree angles. Instead cut the first piece to length with a regular 90-degree cut and cope-cut the second piece (see page 25).

Stain first but paint second: Stain molding before you install it. If you want to paint it, install the molding first, then paint.

2 CUT THE MOLDINGS.

Sight down the blade of the saw and slide the molding until the saw will cut just to the scrap side of your mark. Grasp it tightly so it will not slide as you cut it. For a coped joint, cut the end at a 45 degree angle and highlight the profile with your pencil to make it easier to follow with your coping saw. Cut along the profile to make a back bevel cut. Finish taking off the remaining back bevel with a half-round rasp until the piece sits squarely against your first piece with no gap.

For a scarf joint, cut the first molding's end at 45 degrees. Cut at a 45-degree angle on the next piece to mate with the first. Test-fit the joint.

3 PREDRILL.

Predrill through both sides of a scarf joint. Prevent splitting by driving the nails ½ inch from the top and bottom of the molding. Slightly offset the nails at each stud location.

4 GLUE THE JOINT.

Apply glue to connecting ends to strengthen the joint. Drive finishing nails to hold.

⑤ WORK AROUND THE ROOM.

Continue to measure, cut, and install base molding around the room. When you get to an outside corner, set the first piece a bit long on the wall and mark it by setting your try square or combination square at the corner. Mark the second piece the same way. Miter the ends and check that they meet neatly. If the joint is open at either the top or the bottom, trim each piece with a block plane or resaw it with a playing card between the piece and the saw fence to slightly change the angle. Install the moldings and set the nails below the surface.

⑥ FILL HOLES.

Fill nail holes with wood filler. For stained or clear-finished baseboards, use filler that matches the wood. White filler is fine on painted woodwork. Some fillers shrink as they dry; you may need to wait and apply a second coat of filler.

⑦ INSTALL SHOE MOLDING.

Clean up with sandpaper. To hide the joint, install shoe molding at the bottom of the baseboard.

ACHIEVE THAT PROFESSIONAL LOOK

Avoid splits. Thin stock and moldings are prone to splitting and cracking. Don't take chances. Wherever you will be driving a nail within 3 inches of the edge of a piece, drill a pilot hole. You also can lightly blunt the tip of the nail by hitting it with the hammer. The blunted point will cut and tear through the wood fibers instead of wedging between them and splitting the wood.

The most common mistake when installing molding is using too many nails. Drive in only as many as you need to firmly hold the piece flush against the wall.

INSTALLING CROWN MOLDING

Transform a boxy room with the elegance and beauty of crown molding. With more and more molding profiles available, you have plenty of options for adding an attractive finishing touch to your home.

Although installing crown molding takes patience and a few tricks of the trade, homeowners who are comfortable with basic carpentry tools and who have coped molding joints before should have few problems. Careful fitting and refitting are crucial to obtaining a close fit between sections of molding.

When buying trim, look for straight, solid pieces. Avoid warped or twisted pieces. Measure your wall lengths before purchasing trim. Whenever possible, purchase long enough pieces to avoid cuts.

Select from either softwood or hardwood species. You will find softwoods such as pine, fir, and spruce affordable and easy to work with. Hardwoods such as oak and maple tend to be more expensive and harder to work with. To color match, pick molding from the same bundle at one store. Molding comes in stain-grade and paint-grade. Paint-grade molding is usually shorter pieces finger-jointed together, while stain-grade comes in continuous long pieces.

Store materials in the room you plan to trim. Let the wood set a couple of days to adjust to the environment to avoid shrinkage problems later. Consider selecting trim that is primed on both sides, or prime it yourself.

When working over your head, a solid working platform makes all the difference. Do the careful fitting and nailing that crown molding requires from the ground rather than a stepladder. Make the job easier on yourself by finding a couple of planks and two sturdy sawhorses to make a platform to stand on while installing the molding. In addition, enlist a helper to hold the lengths of molding while you measure, position, and fasten them.

Before beginning this challenging project, review marking and measuring techniques (pages 106–108), how to use a miter box (page 116), and nailing techniques (pages 131–132).

1 START WITH A SQUARE CUT.

To achieve a mitered look in corners that are seldom perfectly square, run the first piece of crown molding tightly into the corners. Cope the mating piece for the corner in the shape of the profile of the molding so it butts neatly against the face of the first piece.

CAUTION

Remember to think upside down as you make miter cuts. Double-check which edge of the crown molding goes up— the difference is subtle.

YOU'LL NEED

TIME: About 4 hours to install crown molding in a 12×12 room.

SKILLS: Measuring precisely, cutting molding with miter box or mitersaw, coping cuts, nailing.

TOOLS: Tape measure, miter box with backsaw or power mitersaw, coping saw, utility knife, hammer, nail set.

BE SHARP

The right tools—kept clean and sharp—help make a precise job, such as installing crown molding, easier. Here are some tips:

Drop off your saw for professional sharpening well before you begin the job. A sharpened saw provides better control and a cleaner cut, and is easier to use.

Buy new coping-saw blades. They break easily, so have half a dozen on hand.

Have plenty of clamps to hold the molding while you cut it. The less you rely on your own holding power, the easier and more accurately you'll be able to make the saw cuts.

2 MAKE A MITER CUT.

Start coping the molding with a miter cut that highlights the molding profile. Use a deep miter box and a fine-tooth backsaw or a power mitersaw. Position the molding so that it is upside down in the miter box. The face of the molding that goes against the ceiling will be on the bottom of the miter box. For inside corners, the bottom of the crown molding will be the longest edge.

3 COPE THE PROFILE.

If the mitered cut is correct, you'll be able to see the profile of the molding. Cut away the wood along the back side of the molding with a coping saw. Err on the side of removing too much rather than too little; only the outermost edge of the coped molding will be seen.

4 FINE-TUNE YOUR CUT.

Use a utility knife or rasp to remove any excess material you missed with the coping saw. Be careful that you do not cut into the exposed face of the molding. Hold the piece in place to test the fit. Take it down and do more trimming if necessary.

5 PLAN EACH JOINT.

Map out the job so that one end of each piece of crown molding always will be cut straight and one end will be mitered and coped. Use butt joints for long runs. Save the most visible parts of the job for last, when you've honed your mitering, coping, and fitting skills.

Installing crown molding (continued)

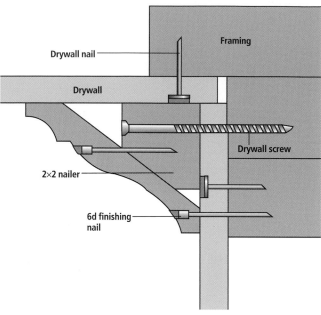

6 NAIL IN PLACE …

If the molding runs perpendicular to the ceiling joists, determine the location of the joists. Drill pilot holes to keep the molding from splitting. As you attach the molding, tack it in place with a few nails. Take a good look at the positioning before completing the nailing.

OR ADD A NAILER.

To provide a solid nailing area where the joists run parallel to the crown molding, cut a beveled face on a 2×2, as shown. Cut the 2×2 to length and screw it to the wall so it's in the corner formed by the ceiling and the wall. The 2×2 provides a surface, at the proper angle, to which you can nail the molding.

PRACTICE MAKES PERFECT

To avoid expensive mistakes with crown molding, hone your mitering and coping skills before you plunge into the job. Buy extra molding of the type you plan to use and cut a 2- or 3-foot piece for test cuts. Practice the steps shown on these pages.

It is particularly important to gain some familiarity with the way molding is cut and coped. The more proficient you are at making overlapping joints, the less likely you are to make costly errors.

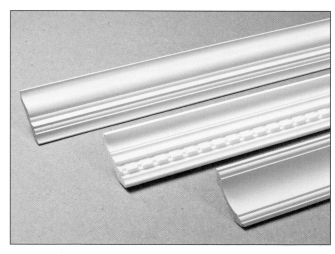

PLASTIC MOLDING ALTERNATIVE

Synthetics have arrived as a wood alternative. The pieces will not shrink or warp the way some wood does, but can look wavy if not supported well. Manufacturers offer a variety of styles. You will find plastic trim lightweight and easy to cut and install. As with wood moldings, you can purchase corner pieces, eliminating miter cuts.

PLANNING FOR NEW CABINETS

You can give old cabinets a new look by painting them and replacing the doors and hardware. Or you can hire a company that specializes in applying new finishes. Often, however, the best solution is to install new cabinets. With careful planning and modest carpentry skills, you can install new kitchen cabinets yourself.

When designing a kitchen, measure your space exactly and map out a wall plan on a piece of graph paper. As you plan, allow an extra inch or so for the width of the stove or refrigerator and for overhead clearance. Make sure that all cabinet doors, as well as those on the dishwasher and range, can open freely.

Many people prefer to have a soffit—a partial wall—coming down from the ceiling to meet the top of the wall cabinets. Building soffits is a lot of work; consider topping off wall cabinets with crown molding instead (see pages 24–26).

Unless you're a real stickler for symmetry, there's no reason to make the wall cabinets the same width as the base cabinets. Your cabinet supply center will have someone to help you design a new layout.

As you plan for new cabinets, upgrade the rest of your kitchen as well. With the old cabinets gone, it's an ideal time to add electrical outlets, under-cabinet lights, flooring, and new plumbing. Patch and paint your walls too.

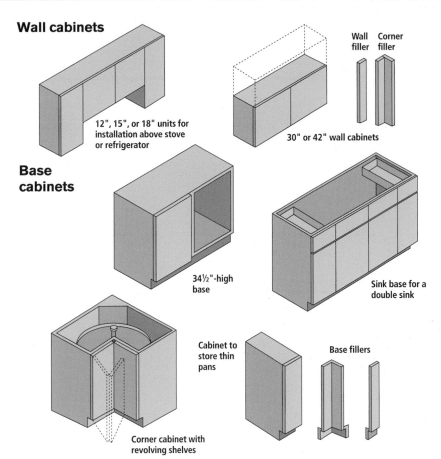

Wall cabinets

12", 15", or 18" units for installation above stove or refrigerator

Wall filler   Corner filler

30" or 42" wall cabinets

Base cabinets

34½"-high base

Sink base for a double sink

Cabinet to store thin pans

Base fillers

Corner cabinet with revolving shelves

SELECT FROM MANY CABINET TYPES.

Ready-made cabinets come in standard sizes that vary in 3-inch increments, so chances are you will need to buy filler pieces to make up gaps of 1 to 3 inches. Base cabinets are typically 24 inches deep and 34½ inches tall; once you add the countertop, your surface will be 36 inches high. Wall cabinets are usually 12 inches deep and 30 or 42 inches tall; some are shorter to fit above stoves, refrigerators, and other appliances. Special base cabinets are available for corners or to hold sinks.

CHOOSING CABINETS

Most manufacturers have several lines of cabinets, each priced according to the quality of materials used in their construction. You can save money by buying unassembled or assembled but unfinished cabinets.

Closely inspect cabinets before buying. The doors should swing freely, latch securely, and line up straight. Drawers should glide on two metal tracks. Adjustable hinges are a plus because doors get out of alignment over time.

Particleboard and hardboard cabinets often come with hardwood or plastic veneers; once scratched, these are difficult to repair. Screws driven into particleboard do not hold well, and hinges can come loose.

Although more expensive, hardwood is the best choice for doors, frames, and sides. It holds up against abuse and can be repaired. When finished properly, hardwood is easy to maintain.

Planning for new cabinets (continued)

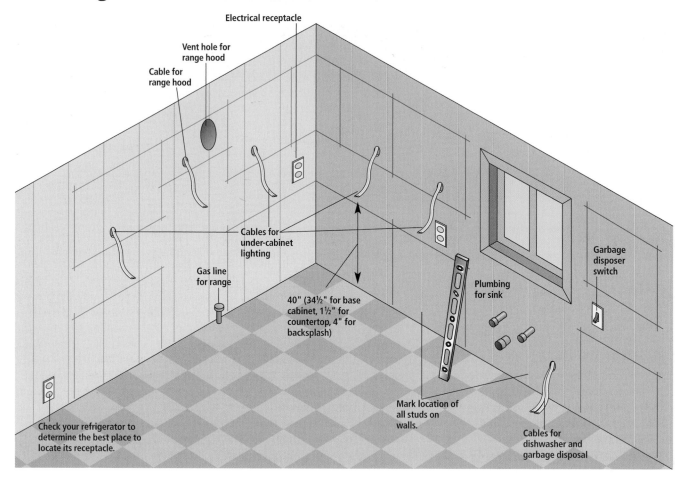

Electrical receptacle

Vent hole for range hood

Cable for range hood

Cables for under-cabinet lighting

Gas line for range

40" (34½" for base cabinet, 1½" for countertop, 4" for backsplash)

Plumbing for sink

Garbage disposer switch

Mark location of all studs on walls.

Cables for dishwasher and garbage disposal

Check your refrigerator to determine the best place to locate its receptacle.

Prepare and lay out walls

Remove the old cabinets. Check your floor for level. If it's off by half an inch or less, you can shim up the base cabinets. If it's way out of level, consider leveling the floor before you install new cabinets. Putting the cabinets over an uneven floor can lead to door and drawer problems. If you will be installing new flooring, it usually is easiest to do it before you install cabinets. Also check your walls for plumb. Depending on which way they lean, you may need to move the cabinets or plan on shimming them plumb.

Start at the highest point of the floor (see page 29) and draw outlines of your base cabinets on the wall. Measure 18 inches up from the cabinet tops and draw outlines of your wall cabinets. A standard kitchen countertop is 36 inches high; the bottom of the wall cabinets should be 54 inches above the floor.

Take a good look at your outlines and visualize how your kitchen will look and work. Use old cabinets or pieces of wood of the same dimensions to get a clear idea of how the cabinets will fit into the space. Now, rather than later, is the best time to change your mind about the cabinet configuration you want. You may want to leave more room around a window or give yourself a couple more inches of traffic space. Be sure that all doors—entry, appliance, and cabinet—will open freely.

Rough in the plumbing and complete the electrical work before installing cabinets. Estimate the wattage demand of your lighting and appliances and plan your electrical circuits to prevent overloading.

Decide where you want electrical receptacles. Be sure to account for the height of the backsplash (4 inches) as well as the countertop when locating outlets. Ground fault circuit

interrupters (GFCIs) are required for all receptacles within 6 feet of a sink. Run wiring for the dishwasher and garbage disposal as well as switches for lights and the garbage disposal.

Plan for under-cabinet lighting. To install fluorescent fixtures under the cabinets, run cable as shown above. Where you poke the cables through the wall depends on how your cabinets are constructed. Or you can install low-voltage halogen lighting after the cabinets are installed.

Buy the range hood and find out where the exhaust hole should go in your wall. Cut the hole and install the ductwork.

Patch the portions of the walls that will show after the cabinets are installed and paint them or hang wallpaper. Make light pencil marks on the walls showing the location of your studs.

INSTALLING BASE CABINETS

Find the highest point of your floor by using a level and a straight 2×4. Start the layout at that point; you can shim cabinets up but not down. Measure up from the high point and snap a level chalk line to show where the tops of the cabinets will go. As you work, take care not to damage the cabinets with your tools. Use screws (most likely supplied by the manufacturer), never nails. If a baseboard or other piece of molding is in the way, remove it and cut it; don't cut the cabinet to fit the molding. If you are installing wall cabinets above the base cabinets, install the wall cabinets first. It is easier to work without the lower ones in the way. Remember to watch your head as you work on the base cabinets.

Base cabinets must be anchored to studs in the kitchen walls just as wall cabinets. Determine where the studs are located in the walls using a stud finder. Remember that studs are normally spaced 16 (or 24) inches apart, so after you find the first one, measure for the rest and verify the location with the stud finder. Mark both edges of each stud.

1 CHECK FOR LEVEL.

Starting at the highest point of the floor, set the first cabinet in place. Check that the cabinet is level from front to back as well as from side to side. Double-check the framing to make certain it is plumb. Shim the bottom of the cabinet if necessary and recheck that the cabinet is level.

Measure the height of the new cabinet. This dimension should be about 34 to 35 inches. Snap a chalk line on the wall along the top of this cabinet to indicate the top edge of the new cabinets.

YOU'LL NEED

TIME: 4 to 6 hours for a medium-size kitchen.

SKILLS: Leveling and plumbing, drilling and driving screws, shimming, clamping.

TOOLS: Tape measure; level; stud finder; hammer; drill with bit set, driver bit, and counterbore bit; nail set; jigsaw with wood-cutting blade; pry bar; clamps.

2 INSTALL THE CORNER CABINET FIRST.

Install the first cabinet in a corner, if possible. Shim the cabinet to position the top level with the line on the wall. Make sure the cabinet is level in all directions. Shim if necessary.

PLAN FOR THE FUTURE

The cabinets you install will be around for years. What may be today's fad may prove to be unbearable to live with or nonfunctional for your style of cooking. Give yourself time. Consider your choices carefully. Just remember the choice you make is one that you will have to live with for 10 years or longer.

3 ATTACH THE CABINET TO THE WALL.

Drill pilot holes and drive in screws through the cabinet framing (not the thin plywood backing) and into wall studs. Wherever the framing is not tight against the wall, use shims to keep the cabinet plumb. Recheck the cabinet for level in both directions before moving on to the next unit. Use a saw or chisel to cut off any protruding shims.

4 JOIN CABINETS TOGETHER.

To ensure tight, even joints between the cabinets, clamp them in place before fastening. Make sure they are flush with each other, not only along their faces, but also at the top. Drill pilot holes for countersunk screws (see page 129), then drive in screws to hold the units together firmly. Attach the cabinet to the wall as you did the first one.

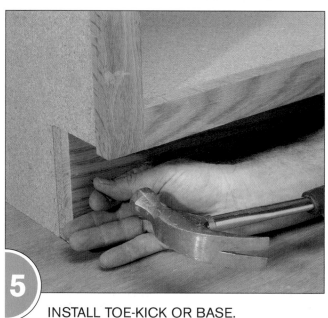

5 INSTALL TOE-KICK OR BASE.

If you have to shim the cabinets, an unsightly gap between the base and the floor may appear. If the toe-kick was preinstalled, remove it by gently prying it off. Reinstall it flush with the floor. Any gap along the top of the toe-kick will be hidden. If the toe-kick was not preinstalled, simply nail it flush with the floor. To dress up the toe-kick, you can put a cove base over it.

HELPFUL TIPS FROM THE PROS

- Think through the process before starting. Draw the cabinet layout to scale for reference throughout the installation process.

- Most stock cabinets are available in 3-inch increments beginning as narrow as 9 inches. Map out your cabinets on graph paper prior to purchasing and installing. Maximize space and minimize filler strips by making slight modifications—within the standard increments—to the widths of your new cabinets.

- Even when you plan to install cabinets yourself, consider hiring a kitchen planner to assist you in planning, designing, and measuring for your new cabinets and other kitchen components. If you do not want to hire a designer, find out if the home center or cabinet dealer offers free measuring services. Precise measurements are essential.

- Be careful during the removal process. Do as little damage as possible to the walls and ceiling.

INSTALLING WALL CABINETS

It's easier to install wall cabinets before base cabinets because you'll have more room to work and lift the cabinets into position. If you do install the base cabinets first, protect them with drop cloths or cardboard while working on the wall cabinets. If you are installing under-cabinet lighting, you may need to drill holes in the wall cabinets for the cable, depending on how the cabinets are constructed.

Cabinets are constructed square and straight. Unfortunately, the same is not always true of kitchen walls. Walls that are not plumb can affect the fit of your cabinets; check for plumb before beginning. Have an abundant supply of shims handy. When properly placed, shims can plumb and level a cabinet despite the irregularity of the wall on which it is mounted.

Install the plumbing and electrical wiring for appliances before installing cabinets. Installing electrical receptacles every 4 feet above the countertop along the backsplash. Rough in cabinet lights and wall-mounted switches. Also mark the locations of all appliances including the vent hood.

Always enlist a helper when installing wall cabinets.

YOU'LL NEED

TIME: 2 to 3 hours for a group of six standard cabinets.

SKILLS: Leveling, drilling, driving screws, shimming.

TOOLS: Tape measure, level, ruler, drill, bit set, chalk line, utility knife, framing square, wood shims, hammer, nail set, clamps, screwdriver bit.

1 ATTACH A TEMPORARY LEDGER.

To ensure that the cabinets align with each other, create a reference line. Use a level to mark a point 54 inches above the highest point on the floor. Snap a chalk line at this mark. Secure a straight board with its top edge along the line, which is where the bottom of your cabinets will be (18 inches above the countertop). Alternatively, make a 2×4 frame of the appropriate height and rest the cabinets on top of it until they are fastened to the wall.

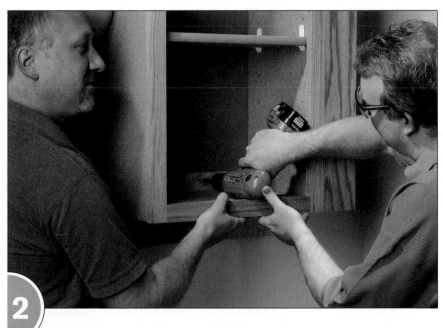

2 ATTACH THE CABINET TO THE WALL.

If the cabinet is heavy, remove shelves and doors to make it manageable. With a helper or two, hold the first cabinet in place. It should rest on top of the guide. Check it for level and plumb. Slip in shims as necessary and drive screws through the top and bottom framing pieces into wall studs. For screw heads that will remain visible, use finish washers. Some manufacturers supply plastic screw-head covers.

Installing wall cabinets *(continued)*

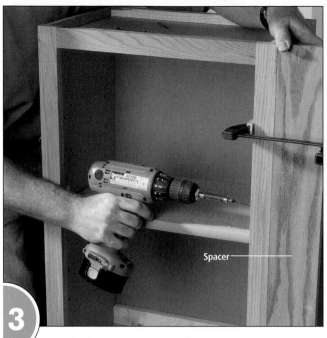

Spacer

3 INSTALL A SPACER AT A CORNER.

In most situations, join wall cabinets together as with base cabinets (see page 30). Spacers can be disguised easily in corners. Begin by attaching the spacer to the cabinet. Rip the spacer to the correct width, clamp it in place, drill and countersink pilot holes, and drive in three screws. Remove the clamps.

MORE HELPFUL PRO TIPS

- If you have a tall cabinet such as a pantry or a built-in oven, use it to determine the height of wall cabinets.

- Allow 4-6 weeks for cabinet delivery. Don't tear out existing cabinets until you know your new cabinets have arrived. Countertops generally take 3-4 weeks for delivery. Order countertops when you order the cabinets.

- Have a plumber and an electrician lined up to rough in new plumbing and electric right after you remove the old cabinets. Plan to have the plumber and electrician return right after you install the countertop.

- If your floors are not level, install base cabinets from the high side of the floor first and work your way to the low side. Shim the cabinets to level as you work. This prevents you from having to cut the underside of any cabinets.

- Use wood clamps to hold cabinets together while you predrill holes through the stiles.

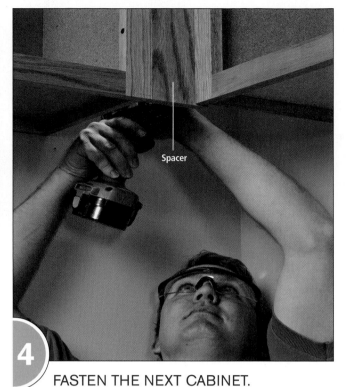

Spacer

4 FASTEN THE NEXT CABINET.

It usually is best not to cover any part of a cabinet frame, or you will have trouble closing cabinet doors. In corners, attach the cabinets by drilling and countersinking pilot holes through the spacer. Drive in screws through the spacer and into the frame of the next cabinet.

Attach a decorative valance above the sink. Clamp in place to the edge of the cabinet. Drill counterbored pilot holes through the cabinet frame into the valance. Fasten with screws.

Using a utility knife, cut all exposed shims flush with the cabinets. Remove the temporary ledger when installation is complete. Trim molding is the perfect way to cover any gaps between the cabinets and walls. Finish by filling holes and sanding. Paint or stain to match the cabinets.

Install the cabinet doors. Check the doors for level and plumb. It may be necessary to adjust the hinges.

CAUTION

SECURE CABINETS TO STUDS.

All that holds wall cabinets up are screws driven into the wall. Stacks of plates and canned goods can add up to some extra-heavy loads, so make sure every cabinet is securely anchored to the wall. Fasteners driven into drywall or plaster alone will not do the job. Screws should go at least 1 inch into wall studs to safely support fully loaded cabinets.

INSTALLING CEILING-HUNG CABINETS

Most people say the kitchen and living room are their favorite places in their home. The idea of the great-room grew from combining these two favorite rooms. Open space is nice, but there's value in maintaining distinct areas for relaxing and cooking. A divider or buffer may be just the solution. Peninsula and ceiling-hung cabinets fill this need. They separate, yet don't isolate, while providing additional work surface and storage.

YOU'LL NEED

TIME: 2 to 3 hours for a group of six standard cabinets.

SKILLS: Leveling, drilling, driving screws, shimming.

TOOLS: Tape measure, level, ruler, drill, bit set, chalk line, utility knife, framing square, wood shims, hammer, nail set, clamps, screwdriver bit.

ADDING CEILING CABINETS.

Whether you call it blocking, bracing, or framing, you'll need it when mounting cabinets to the ceiling for an island or peninsula. It's basically the same as installing cabinets on the wall. The end result is more storage space and an area that brings the kitchen into adjoining rooms, creating a connection between spaces.

1 **SET THE BLOCKING.**

Determine the location of the cabinets. Following the manufacturer's specifications, measure the location of the blocking and attach it to the ceiling joists. If the joists run parallel to the cabinets, you'll need to add 2×4s between the joists to hold the blocking.

2 **ATTACH THE FIRST CABINET TO THE BLOCKING.**

Place the cabinet and drive screws into the blocking to secure the cabinet in place.

3 **LEVEL THE NEXT CABINET.**

Have a helper assist by holding the next cabinet in place. Make sure that the cabinet is plumb and level; otherwise the door will not shut properly. Few things are as annoying as a cabinet that pops open on its own after you close it.

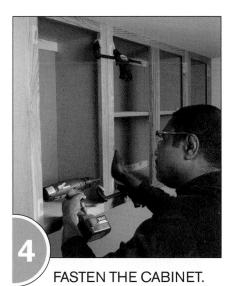

4 **FASTEN THE CABINET.**

It usually is best not to cover any part of a cabinet frame, or you will have trouble closing cabinet doors. In corners, attach the cabinets by drilling and countersinking pilot holes through a spacer. Drive screws through the spacer into the frame of the next cabinet.

COUNTERTOP IDEAS

Laminate countertops have evolved in both durability and design. The gold-flecked white surface that would scratch at the drop of a knife and the metal strip nailed over the edge are long gone. Unless you want a retro look, self edging has replaced the metal strips, and durability has substantially improved. For added elegance, you can even incorporate wood and other laminate colors or textures in edging. Current laminate countertops can provide the beauty and durability of more-expensive materials at a fraction of the cost.

ALMOST ENDLESS VARIETY
Laminate countertops are now available in myriad patterns, colors, and textures, making them a versatile and affordable choice. This laminate bathroom countertop resembles natural wood. Stone-look laminate finishes are also popular.

NEUTRAL TOP FITS ANY DESIGN
The neutral color of this laminate countertop works well with the natural tones throughout the kitchen. Laminate is strong and easy to clean, but it can chip. Care should be taken during installation and use.

ALTERNATIVE COUNTERTOP MATERIALS

Solid granite countertops are expensive, but they look great and will last forever. Man-made composite countertops, such as Corian and Avonite, also are extremely durable and come in a wide choice of colors and patterns. In most cases, granite or composite tops should be fabricated and installed by professionals.

If you have tiling experience, you can cover a countertop with ceramic or granite tile. Begin with a solid, level plywood or backerboard base. Set ceramic tiles in tile adhesive or thinset mortar. Set granite tiles in silicone caulk. Your tile dealer can supply you with cutters, adhesives, and grout for both types of materials.

INSTALLING A COUNTERTOP

Countertops covered with plastic laminate are durable and economical; thus, they are the most common choice. (See *opposite* for other options.) If your layout is straightforward, you can buy a ready-made, postformed top, which has a curved front lip and an integrated backsplash. Factory-cut miters make corners easy to handle. Or you can laminate or order your own square-edged top. Analyze the situation carefully. If your walls are more than ⅜ inch out of square or the kitchen layout is complex, you may need to consult a countertop professional.

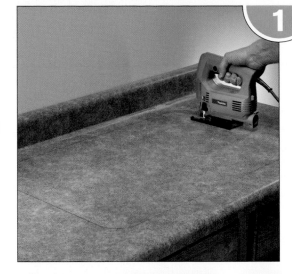

1 CUT THE TOP.

To make a sink cutout, mark the top according to manufacturer's directions; usually the hole should be 1 inch smaller than the outside dimensions of the sink. Use a jigsaw with a fine-tooth, downcut blade. To cut a ready-made top to length, turn it upside down and use a circular saw with a straightedge guide. Support the scrap carefully or the laminate will crack.

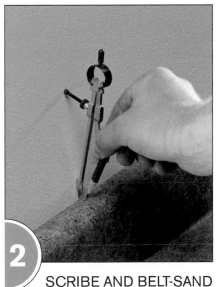

2 SCRIBE AND BELT-SAND THE BACKSPLASH.

Most tops have a ⅜-inch lip at the top of the backsplash that you can cut to accommodate wavy or out-of-square walls. Set the top into place against the wall and scribe the wall contour on the backsplash by running a compass along the wall. Don't try to cut off excess material; it will crack. Instead use a belt sander to carefully remove the material.

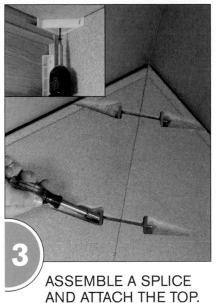

3 ASSEMBLE A SPLICE AND ATTACH THE TOP.

Butt the pieces together on top of the base cabinets. Working from underneath, tighten the supplied bolts. Check the top as you work to make sure the splice is flat and the ends are even. To fasten the top in place (inset), drive screws up through the cabinet framing. Screws should be long enough to hold the top but not so long as to pierce the surface.

4 ATTACH END CAPS.

For each exposed edge, buy an end cap (either left-hand or right-hand). To attach the end cap, warm it in the oven or use a household iron to melt the glue as you press it into place. Make sure all countertop edges are covered. After the cap is cool, use a router with a flush-trimming bit or a file to remove the excess material and form a uniform edge.

YOU'LL NEED

TIME: 2 to 3 hours to scribe and install a medium-size top.

SKILLS: Precise measuring and cutting, scribing, fastening.

TOOLS: Circular saw or jigsaw, belt sander, wrenches, router, iron, drill.

ORGANIZING A BEDROOM CLOSET

A typical closet with a single hanging pole and one or two long shelves wastes a lot of space and is difficult to use. Your clothing will fit without wasted space and you can easily get at the things you frequently need if you treat your closet to custom organizers.

You can buy ready-made storage or shelf units that are easy to install, build your own shelves and dividers out of lumber, or use a combination of the two. Keep in mind that painting wood shelves often is more time-consuming than building them.

GROUP FOR EFFICIENCY AND ORGANIZATION.

Once you've installed the custom-built closet organizer system, group clothes according to length, type, season, and color. By grouping like types of clothing, you can quickly find what you want.

PLAN A WELL-ORGANIZED CLOSET

Measure and catalog your clothes and storage items (see the chart below for some standard sizes). By grouping clothes according to height, you can gain usable space. Measure the horizontal space needed for each type of clothing. Make a sketch of your ideal finished closet, taking into account the ¾-inch thickness of boards.

Sometimes it makes sense to begin with a set of store-bought drawers and build shelves around it. Be sure the closet pole is well-supported every 4 feet or in time it will sag.

Decide which storage items can be placed up high. Avoid tall stacks of clothes and use storage boxes or wire bins where possible.

ATTACH THE SHELF SUPPORTS.

Measure and mark the location of the top and bottom shelf supports on the back wall and sidewalls of the closet. A good height for the top shelf is 84 inches above the floor; for the bottom shelf, 76 inches. This provides plenty of storage room between the two shelves without making the top shelf unreachable. Mark the locations on the walls with a chalk line. Determine the locations of the wall studs using a stud finder and mark them. Studs will provide support. Drive 8d finishing nails through the supports into the wall studs.

1

YOU'LL NEED

TIME: For a typical 6-foot closet, one day to build an organizer.

SKILLS: Measuring and cutting, fastening with screws or nails.

TOOLS: Circular saw, tape measure, framing square, stud finder, chalk line, hammer, nail set, drill and screwdriver bit.

CLOTHING DIMENSIONS

Women's Item	Length	Men's Item	Length	Accessories	Length
Long dresses	69"	Topcoats	50"	Garment bags	57"
Robes	52"	Trousers (cuff-hung)	44"	Hanging shoe bags	36"
Coats	52"	Travel bags	41"	Umbrellas and canes	36"
Dresses	45"	Suits	38"		
Skirts	29"	Shirts	28"		
Suits	29"	Ties	27"		
Blouses	28"	Trousers (double-hung)	20"		

2 ASSEMBLE THE CENTER SHELF UNIT.

Space the center shelves evenly or space them according to your design plan. It may be advantageous to vary the shelf heights depending on the items you are storing. Drive 6d finishing nails to hold the shelves in place. Be sure to leave the top and bottom units open.

4 SET THE TOP SHELF.

Drive 6d finishing nails through the shelf into the center shelf to hold it in place. Once attached, set the top shelf.

PRECUT MATERIALS.

It may be easier to precut your materials and have them ready for installation. This requires careful planning and accurate measurements. Measure and draw to scale your new closet on a piece of graph paper. For this project materials were precut.

3 POSITION THE CENTER SHELF UNIT.

Position the center shelf unit either at the middle of the closet or where it best fits your needs. You could offset the unit to provide more storage room on one side of the closet. Mark the location. Make sure that the top of the shelf unit is flush with the top of the lower shelf support bracket. If it is not, mark to cut so it is flush. Mark the top for a notch to fit over the lower shelf support. Remove the shelf and cut the notch with a circular saw or jigsaw. Align the center shelf unit with the mark. Check for level. Have a helper hold it in place while you set the lower shelf on top of the lower shelf support.

5 INSTALL POLE BRACKETS.

Measure for location of pole brackets on shelf unit and mark. Install pole brackets on whichever side of the center shelf you desire at a height of 38 inches above the floor for a lower clothes pole. Attach pole bracket to stud at opposite end wall of the closet, 3 inches from the bottom of the lower shelf. Attach pole brackets to center shelf unit with screws.

BUILDING SHELVES

You can build the simple dadoed shelf unit shown *opposite* easily, altering the dimensions to fit your needs. Though the project is relatively easy, you must be careful when measuring and cutting. The mitered corners need to fit tightly for strength and appearance. Making straight cuts is difficult if the boards are warped or bowed, so choose the straightest boards you can find. The end result, a unit custom-made for your space, will be worth the effort.

YOU'LL NEED

TIME: 2 hours to make the project shown on this page.

SKILLS: Precise measuring and cutting, fastening.

TOOLS: Circular saw, tablesaw, or radial-arm saw; speed square; pencil; hammer; chisel; strap clamp.

1 CUT THE SIDES, TOP, AND BOTTOM.

Cut 45-degree bevels on both ends of the two sides, the top, and the bottom. Be sure the saw is set accurately to a 45-degree bevel; make test cuts on scrap wood. Use a tablesaw or a radial-arm saw or hold a speed square firmly against a factory edge as you cut with a circular saw. Measure from outside to outside—from the tip of one cut to the tip of the next.

2 CUT THE DADOES.

Set the two vertical outside pieces side by side and mark them for the ¾-inch dadoes. Set the depth of your saw blade so it cuts ¼ inch deep. Make a series of cuts (see pages 143–144). Clean out the dadoes by cutting out remaining wood with a chisel, then smooth the bottom with the chisel held bevel side down.

3 MEASURE FOR THE SHELVES.

Temporarily fasten the box together by drilling pilot holes and partially driving (tacking) finishing nails at each corner. Or use a strap clamp (see page 139). Check the box for square. Measure from the inside of each dado to inside of the corresponding dado to determine the length of each shelf. Cut the shelves to length.

4 ASSEMBLE THE PIECES.

Disassemble the box. Apply glue and drive the nails that hold one side piece to the top and bottom pieces. Carefully position these fastened pieces so the side piece is lying on a flat surface. Dry-fit the shelves into the dadoes and set the remaining side piece in place. Disassemble and make any needed adjustments. Apply glue, check for square, and nail.

5 ADD THE BACK.

Cut a piece of ¼-inch plywood or ⅛-inch hardboard for the back. It should be ¼ inch smaller than the outside dimensions of the unit, so the backing edge is ⅛ inch inside the outer edge. Use the back to check that the unit is square. Leaving a ⅛-inch gap on all edges, fasten with 4d box nails every 4 inches. Fasten the back to the inner shelves as well.

CHOOSE ADJUSTABLE OR FIXED SHELVING.

When building a shelf system using adjustable standards and clips and a central vertical support, the adjustable shelves must be shorter than the top and bottom. For a cleaner look, set the metal standards in grooves. To make pin-type adjustable shelves, precisely lay out the locations of the holes on the side pieces by clamping the sides together before marking. Use a sharp bit (hollow-point bits work well) that will not chip the surface of the wood as you bore the holes. If a pin-type adjustable shelf unit is taller than 4 to 5 feet, it should have one or more fixed shelves to keep the side pieces from bowing out. You can add an angle bracket or wooden cleat to which you can attach the fixed shelf.

The simplest unit has shelves screwed in place without dadoes. Such a unit is quite strong, as long as you use three or more screws at each joint and the screws are fastened firmly. Drill pilot holes to avoid splitting the wood. Countersink the screw heads and fill the holes with putty or plugs (see pages 129–130). If you use trim head screws, the holes will not be much larger than those for finishing nails. To make such shelves even stronger, add cleats.

A cleat-supported shelf is simple to build and ideal for utility areas. Use 1×2s for the cleats. Cut the front edge of each cleat at a 45-degree angle so it's not as noticeable. Secure the cleat with countersunk screws.

Dadoed shelves are stronger and present a clean, finished look because there is no hardware to hide. (See page 38 for how to build this unit.)

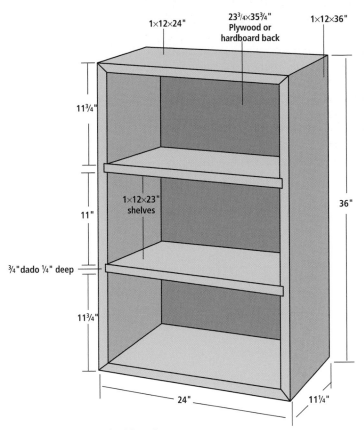

Dadoed shelf unit

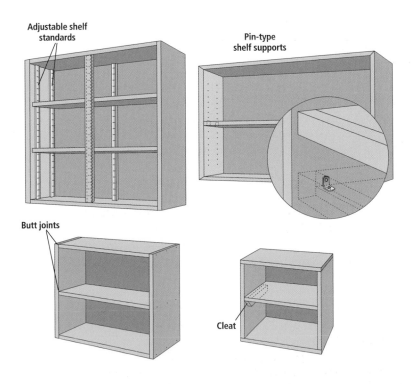

HANGING SHELVES AND CABINETS

Any shelf system, be it simple boards or a cabinet with doors, must hang securely on a wall. If it is not anchored into wall studs, it probably will come loose when weight is put on it. If it is not plumb and level, it will look shoddy and may even prove unsafe. As you plan your shelving, decide the following:

Will the shelves be supported at their ends (by the side of the shelf unit or cabinet) or from the back?

Do you want the shelves to be adjustable or fixed? Shelves in living areas require the versatility of adjustable hardware; utility shelves used for storage in closets, garages, and basements are fine with fixed supports.

Select the hardware that suits your purposes best. The chart below shows the most common options.

To make sure the shelves won't sag over time, use the span chart (below

left) to determine the correct distance between shelf supports. The spacings listed assume shelves are fully loaded with books—most likely the heaviest load they'll have to bear.

If you opt for fixed shelves, measure the tallest items slated to go on the shelves and add at least 1 inch for overhead clearance.

SHELF HARDWARE OPTIONS

Item	Application
	Rigid pressed-steel angle brackets hold medium-weight loads. For heavier loads, choose types reinforced with triangular gussets. Mount with the longer leg against the wall. Check that upper screws are fastened firmly.
	Brackets that clip into slotted standards. are the best way to provide adjustable support when you can mount only from the rear. Choose 8-, 10-, or 12-inch brackets.
	For adjustable shelves with a finished appearance, mount shelves on the ends by popping pin-type clips into predrilled holes. The clips are relatively inexpensive, but the holes must be drilled precisely.
	These end-mounted adjustable standards and clips are strong but less attractive than other alternatives. For a dressier look, rabbet the standards into the cabinet sides.
	Light-duty wire brackets are among the many accessories you can mount on perforated hardboard. Measure the thickness of the pegboard before you buy it; 1/4- and 1/8-inch perforated hardboard require different bracket types.

PLANNING YOUR SHELF LAYOUT

- It may seem time-consuming, but you'll thank yourself for drawing a detailed plan of your shelf or cabinet system. Without a plan, it's hard to buy materials and easy to overlook hard-to-correct design flaws.

- Make sure unsupported shelf ends extend no more than one-third the distance between the shelf standards.

- If you settle on fixed shelves, maximize space by tailoring the vertical spacings so your possessions fit exactly. Keep in mind that your shelving needs may change over time. Adjustable shelves offer the most flexibility.

YOU'LL NEED

TIME: About 2 hours to hang an average shelf or cabinet system.

SKILLS: Measuring, plumbing, leveling, driving screws, finding wall studs.

TOOLS: Tape measure, drill, screwdriver, level, stud finder, awl.

SHELVING SPANS

Material Used	Maximum Span	Material Used	Maximum Span
3/4-inch plywood	32"	2×6, 2×8 lumber	36"
3/4-inch particleboard	24"	2×10, 2×12 lumber	48"
1×6, 1×8 lumber	18"	1/2-inch acrylic sheet	18"
1×10, 1×12 lumber	24"	3/8-inch glass	16"

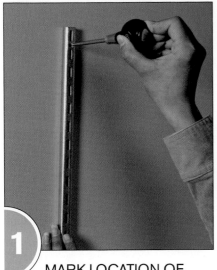

1 MARK LOCATION OF STANDARDS.

Find at least two wall studs to support the shelf standards. To find a stud, tap the wall until you hear a dull, not a hollow, sound. Or use a stud finder. Hammer in a small finishing nail to confirm you've found the stud. Hold one standard at the desired location and height. Mark for the top hole with an awl, then drill a pilot hole.

2 PLUMB AND SECURE THE STANDARD.

Drive in and partially tighten the screw at the top of the standard. Using a carpenter's level, plumb the dangling standard, then use an awl to mark for the bottom hole. Attach the standard, check again that it is plumb, and finish securing it.

3 MARK FOR THE OTHER STANDARDS.

Run a straightedge and level from the top of the standard to the approximate location of the last standard. Strike an erasable line and step back to see if the line looks level. If it doesn't, redraw the line so it's parallel to the floor or ceiling. Install the other standards, making sure their top ends are up.

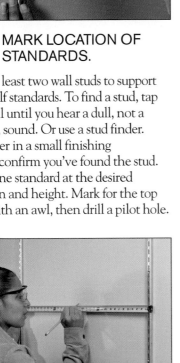

4 INSTALL INTERMEDIATE STANDARDS.

If shelves will bear heavy loads, install intermediate standards to prevent sagging. Mark the position between the end standards. Place a shelf bracket at the same location on both end standards and locate the intermediates by laying a straightedge across the brackets.

MOUNT A CABINET OR SHELF UNIT.

Of the many ways to hang cabinets on walls, the one shown *at right* is one of the best. It provides plenty of holding power without visible screw heads or supports. It's also easy to level; you need only level the back cleat. The back of the unit, however, must be recessed ¾ inch.

Cut a 1×4 to fit behind the cabinet. Make a beveled rip cut along its center line (see pages 116 and 124–125). Attach one of the pieces to the cabinet. Level and secure the other one to the wall. Lift the unit and hold it against the wall, then slide it down onto the piece attached to the wall.

If a cabinet is well-constructed, another approach is to attach it to the wall simply by holding it in place and driving screws through

the cabinet back into wall studs. Place screws where they will be least visible.

DISPLAY COLLECTIBLES
Decorative shelves lend an architectural line to any room while creating a focal point for art and collectibles.

Make the most of wall space with a decorative shelf constructed with trim molding. Set alone to draw the eye or cover a wall to create an architectural statement. Make the shelf deep enough to hold a gallery of framed photographs of family, friends, and cherished pets and small objects. Adjust the depth of the top shelf to 10 inches and go for an eclectic effect by displaying candles, objets d'art, or flowers.

SUIT A MODERN STYLE
Decorative shelves can enhance the look of a modern decorating scheme with minimal effort. Instead of combining various molding to create the molding shelves, cut single pieces of wood to the length of your shelf, *left*.

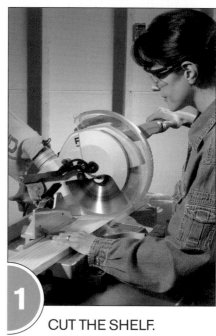

1 CUT THE SHELF.

Use a miter box and backsaw or power mitersaw to cut the length of the top of your shelf. Good lengths are 2, 3, or 4 feet for a shelf. A set of three makes a nice grouping.

2 CUT THE MOLDING.

Cut the molding ends with opposing 45-degree angles. Measure and cut the end pieces to abut the front molding. The sides of the end pieces that fit against the wall should be 90-degree cuts to seat flush against the wall.

3 APPLY GLUE.

Apply wood glue to the surface areas of the molding and the shelf. Attach the front length of the crown molding to the shelf with glue (see pages 138–139).

4 CLAMP TOGETHER.

Drive finishing nails through the crown molding into the top of the shelf. Apply glue to the end pieces and attach flush to the front molding with finishing nails. Set the nails using a nail set.

5 FILL NAIL HOLES.

Fill the nail holes with a wood filler and allow it to dry. If shrinkage occurs, apply more wood filler (see pages 153–154).

6 SAND SMOOTH.

Sand to finish. Start with a coarse-grit sandpaper. Gradually work to a fine-grit sandpaper for a smooth finish (see pages 151–152).

7 FINISH WITH PAINT.

Apply primer for painting, or stain and apply a clear-coat sealant. To install the shelf, locate wall studs with a stud finder. Attach a cleat to the wall and fit the shelf over the cleat. Secure with countersunk screws down through the shelf into the cleat.

SOLVING DOOR PROBLEMS

If a door sticks or does not close properly, don't assume that you need to remove it and plane it. Analyze the situation while the door is in place. Often screws holding the top hinge come loose, causing the door to lean. Remount the screws (see *far right*).

Loose screws, however, may be a symptom of other problems. Close the door, watching the hinge leaf that is connected to the jamb. If the hinge leaf moves, it is under stress and will come loose again. Check where the door is rubbing, scribe a line along it, and plane it.

WHERE'S THE RUB

When a door sticks, it is not always obvious just where the door is rubbing against the jamb. Close the door and insert a piece of cardboard into the gap between the door and the jamb. Slide it until you find a tight spot; that's where the door is sticking. For an exterior door, test the threshold as well.

Before scribing a mark to plane a sticking door (see page 112), close the door to the point where it begins to stick, and no further. If the door is significantly too wide, remove the door and plane it until it closes without straining. Then complete the planing.

YOU'LL NEED

TIME: 1 to 2 hours to diagnose and repair a door.

SKILLS: Close observation, planing, fastening screws.

TOOLS: Screwdriver, hammer, nail set, plane, chisel.

USE CARDBOARD TO SHIM A DOOR.

If your door is rubbing against the jamb on the hinge side, you can relieve the pressure by shimming the hinges out. Unscrew the part of the hinge connected to the jamb and insert a piece of cardboard behind it. If a door binds at the top of the strike jamb, you may be able to fix it by shimming out the bottom hinge.

REMOVE A DOOR.

If your door needs to be modified so it will fit, mark it with clear scribe lines. You probably will need to remove it to get at the edges that need planing. Tap the hinge pins out with a nail set, removing the bottom pin first. If the hinges are old and the pins are solidly rusted or painted in place, unscrew the hinges from the door to remove it.

REMOUNT AND TIGHTEN HINGE SCREWS.

If hinge screws are loose, wedge the door open and remove the screws. Fold back the hinge, taking care not to lose shims that may be behind it. Whittle hole-size pieces of wood or dowels, add carpenter's glue, and push them into the holes. Chisel the plugs flush, fold the hinge back, drill pilot holes, and drive the screws.

PLANE THE DOOR.

To plane the edge, stand the door on its edge on a flat surface. Brace it in a corner so it will stay still as you work. If you need to plane the top or bottom of the door, work from each end toward the middle to avoid splintering at the edges. (see pages 149–150). If you have to shorten a door, say to clear new carpeting, cut the door with a circular saw, then plane it smooth.

MOVE THE STOP TO CORRECT A BIND.

Sometimes a door will bind against the stop on the hinge side, or it will not close properly because the stop on the latch side is placed improperly. In either case, it is easier to move the stop than to unwarp a door. Pry the stop off. Close the door and scribe a line on the jamb along the door's edge. Nail the stop on this line.

SHIM A STRIKE PLATE.

If a strike plate is too far away for the door latch to engage it, shim it out with cardboard. Often a latch and strike will get out of alignment because the house has settled. If this occurs, unscrew the strike, chisel out a new mortise, drill pilot holes, and reinstall the strike. Fill the old mortise cavity with wood putty and sand it smooth.

QUIETING SQUEAKS

Rusty hinges may cause door squeaks. Solving noisy door problems may be simple. Before removing the door or the hinges, open the door and oil the hinges with lightweight oil. Then open and close the door several times.

If the oil did not solve the problem, prop open the door with shims at the floor and remove a hinge pin. Clean rust off the hinge pin and clean out the pinholes in the hinge, using a pipe cleaner or rolled-up emery cloth. Oil the parts and replace the hinge pin. Repeat this process for the other hinge(s). Do not tap the hinge pins all the way down; leave a little gap so they can be pried out easily. Still squeaking? Replace the hinges.

CUTTING A DOOR

To avoid splintering the door face, score a line with a knife wherever you will be cutting across the grain on a panel door. Then make your saw cut below that line with a smooth-cutting blade.

Newer, solid-core doors are filled with particleboard; there is solid wood for only about an inch around the perimeter. If you cut more than an inch, the exposed particleboard will require a couple of coats of sealer.

Trimming a hollow-core door is more complex (see steps, *right*).

YOU'LL NEED

TIME: About 2 hours to cut down a hollow-core door.

SKILLS: Measuring, cutting a straight line, smoothing.

TOOLS: Knife, circular saw, straightedge, chisel, hammer.

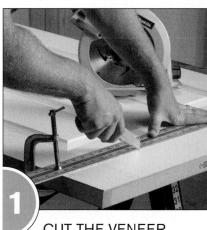

1 CUT THE VENEER, THEN THE DOOR.

With a straightedge clamped in position, cut through the veneer with a sharp utility knife about 1/16 inch above where you want your final cut. It may take several passes with your knife to do this. Move the straightedge into final position, clamp it, and complete the cut with a circular saw (see page 114).

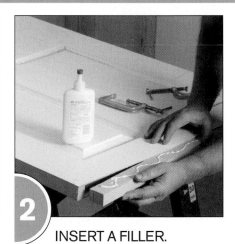

2 INSERT A FILLER.

If you cut off more than two inches of a hollow-core door, the door will be hollow at the place you just cut. Clear out some of the cardboard webbing with a chisel. Rip a piece of softwood to the required width and length. Apply carpenter's glue to both sides of the piece and tap it into position. Clamp firmly until the glue has set.

INSTALLING DOOR HINGES

A door that swings easily on neatly installed hinges is the hallmark of a good carpenter. Hanging a door requires care and patience. If you work carefully and pay attention to details, you can install a door that swings freely and shuts firmly.

If you are replacing an old door, the door opening may not be square. Most homes settle over the years, causing door openings to become out of square. Cutting the door to fit the opening will be the first and most difficult task. If the old door fits well, use it as a template. Simply remove the old hardware, lay the door on top of your new door, and trace around it for trimming. If the old door did not fit well, have a helper hold the new door in place while you shim it into final position. Carefully mark trimming points. If the door jamb is damaged and must be replaced, take care to square the new jamb as you install it. Or install a prehung door (page 49).

Hanging a door involves a strict order. First hang the door and make sure it swings freely and closes tightly against the doorstop. Next install the lockset. Finally cut the hole for and install the strike plate.

YOU'LL NEED

TIME: About 3 hours to hang a door and install a new lockset and deadbolt.

SKILLS: Measuring precisely, chiseling, drilling, fastening with screws.

TOOLS: Drill with the correct bits (check the lockset instructions), utility knife or butt marker, tape measure, center punch, screwdriver, hammer, chisel, awl.

1 MARK THE HINGE LOCATIONS.

Leave half of the hinge on the door jamb. Set the door in place, using shims to wedge it exactly in place. Make sure the gaps at the bottom and the top of the door are even. With a pencil or a knife, carefully mark the location of the hinges by marking the bottom and top of each hinge.

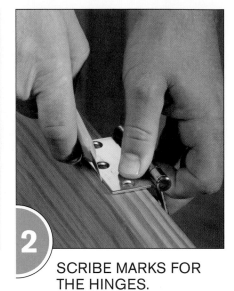

2 SCRIBE MARKS FOR THE HINGES.

Mark the outline of the hinges by holding the hinge in place as a template. Use a utility knife to make a light mark around each hinge. A handy tool called a butt marker has chisel edges that will make indentations for a perfect cut. Hold it in place and tap it with a hammer.

3 CHISEL THE MORTISE.

With a knife or a chisel, deepen the lines marking the outside edges of the hinge until they are the full depth of the mortise. Holding the chisel with the beveled edge down, cut away enough material so that the hinge half sits flush with the surface of the door edge.

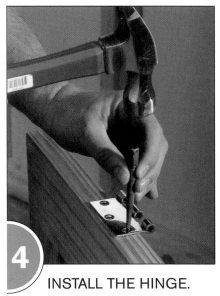

4 INSTALL THE HINGE.

Remove the pin from the hinge and install the separate halves on the door and jamb. Position a hinge half in its mortise and mark it for drilling with a center punch. Be careful to drill straight pilot holes so the screw heads sit flush. Drive screws into all the holes. Hang the door by aligning the hinge sections and reinserting the pin.

INSTALLING LOCKSETS

1 MARK HOLES.

Locksets or deadbolts come with paper or cardboard templates to help position them on the door. If a strike plate exists in the jamb, align the template with it so you won't have to cut a new mortise. If not, place the lock 36 inches from the floor. Tape or hold the template against the door, as shown. With an awl or the point of a spade bit, mark for the holes in the door face and edge by piercing through the template.

2 DRILL THE HOLES.

Drill the hole through the face of the door first, using a holesaw. To avoid splintering the veneer, drill just far enough so the pilot bit of the holesaw pokes through the other side. Then drill from the other side. Use a spade bit to drill through the edge; be sure to hold the bit parallel to the surface of the door and perpendicular to its edge. Some locksets require that you continue drilling into the rear of the large hole another half inch.

3 MORTISE THE LATCH BOLT.

Insert the bolt through the smaller hole and hold it centered in the door while you mark for its mortise. Use a sharp pencil or a knife to mark the outline. Cut and chisel a mortise as you did for the hinges (see page 46). Depending on the type of bolt, the mortise may need to be deeper near the center than at the edges.

4 INSTALL THE BOLT AND HANDLES.

Install the bolt by setting it in the mortise, drilling pilot holes, and driving the screws provided. Install the lockset or handles according to the manufacturer's directions. Tighten all screws. Test the mechanisms to make sure they operate smoothly; you may need to clean out or widen your holes.

5 INSTALL THE STRIKE PLATE.

Mark the jamb for the correct location of the strike plate. The latch or bolt should be centered vertically in the strike opening.and should enter the door jamb. Mortise the jamb, drill pilot holes, and install the strike with the screws provided.

SELECT THE CORRECT DRILL BITS

Most lockset manufacturers call for a 2⅛-inch hole in the face of the door and a ⅞-inch hole in the door edge. But don't take that for granted; when you buy the handle or lockset, check the instructions and buy the right drill bits at the same time.

A standard holesaw works best for the large hole. An adjustable hole cutter will work, but it is harder to use successfully to bore through a door. It will cut more slowly and may result in a rougher cut, but you can use it for different sizes of holes on other projects.

A spade bit works fine for the smaller hole, but if you want a more precise cut, use a Forstner bit.

INSTALLING A DEADBOLT LOCK

Deadbolt locks add security to a door. These locks have long bolts that reach into the jamb and sometimes into the framing.

A double-cylinder deadbolt, which locks with a key on the inside as well as the outside, offers the best security in situations where an intruder could reach through a broken or forced window to unlock the thumb turn on a single-cylinder deadbolt locks. However, it is not safe in case of fire—if you don't have the key handy, you could be stuck inside.

When purchasing a deadbolt, look for these features:

The bolt should extend 1 inch or more in length at full extension. This ensures a degree of strength against forced entry.

The collar surrounding the bolt should be of substantial construction.

Install a strike plate to the frame to give the bolt a strong anchor in which to seat.

YOU'LL NEED

TIME: About 1 hour.

SKILLS: Drilling holes, mortising, assembling parts.

TOOLS: Drill with the required bits, chisel, knife.

1 DRILL HOLES AND CUT MORTISE.

Following the same techniques as for a lockset (see page 47), mark the position of the two holes and drill them, taking care to hold the drill perpendicular to the door. Insert the bolt and latch face into their hole and mark for the mortise with a sharp knife. Cut the mortise with a chisel (see page 46).

2 ASSEMBLE THE LOCK.

Screw the latch face into the mortise. For many lock types, you'll need to use a screwdriver to partially extend the bolt. Insert the lock tailpiece through the slot in the bolt mechanism and slip on the interior turn bolt or lock until the two pieces sit flush against the door. Fasten the retaining screws. Install the strike plate.

FRENCH AND PATIO DOOR SECURITY RETROFIT

Historically less secure than single doors, French and patio sliding doors need not be the weak point in your home security. Newer installations have two- and three-point locking systems that secure the doors at the top, bottom, and latch. However, you don't need to replace your old doors to gain the added security of the new French doors.

If both doors open inward, fit the doors with rack bolts. Mount the locks 90 degrees to the wood grain. This will reduce the potential of the wood splintering when subjected to forced pressure.

If your French door opens outward, a hinge lock provides the security that a rack bolt won't.

Fit patio doors with a patio lock that attaches to the bottom of the fixed frame. These locks push through to the sliding door frame in the center and on the side frame. Push these types to lock and key them to open.

Rack bolts can be installed on patio doors. However, they are often left unlocked, defeating the purpose.

High-strength plastic glazing and laminated safety glass are harder to break out than tempered glass.

INSTALLING A PREHUNG DOOR

A prehung door costs a little more than buying a door, a doorjamb kit, and the trim separately. But it will save you a lot of time and may result in a better installation. With a prehung door, you'll avoid having to cut the jamb, three stop pieces, and six casing pieces; mortise and install hinges; and drill and mortise for the handle and the strike plate.

Test-fit the prehung door unit in the rough opening. Check the hinge-side jamb for plumb and the jamb head for level. If the jamb head isn't level, raise whichever jamb side will make it level. Measure the distance between the bottom of the raised jamb side and the floor, then shorten the other jamb side by that amount.

Tack the hinge-side jamb into the rough opening. Attach a plumb bob to the top of the hinge-side jamb. Use a tape measure or ruler to measure the gap between the string and the jamb at several points, and plumb the jamb side. Slide overlapping pairs of shims into the gaps between the jamb and the rough opening at the top, bottom, and middle and at each hinge location. Adjust the shim thickness to plumb the jamb side. Nail the jamb to the framing through the shims. Trim off the shim ends with a saw or utility knife so they are flush with the surface.

Shim and nail the head jamb to the header in the rough opening. The gap between the top of the door

INSTALL A STANDARD PREHUNG DOOR.

Set the door into the opening and shim it, if necessary, to plumb it. Temporarily attach the hinge side of the jamb to the framing. Check the other two jamb pieces for square with a framing square and by closing the door; the gap should be even all around. Shim as necessary and attach all sides of the jamb. Install the casing.

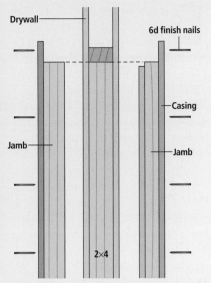

INSTALL A SPLIT-JAMB PREHUNG DOOR.

With this type of prehung door, the jamb is split, and the casing remains attached to the two jamb halves. Install the jamb half that has the door attached, just as you would a standard prehung door. Slip in the second half and cover the joint between the two with the stop molding provided.

and the head jamb should be uniform from left to right and $\frac{1}{8}$ to $\frac{3}{16}$ inch wide, about the same as the space on the hinge side of the jamb.

Attach the latch-side jamb to the framing. The gap between the door and the jamb on the latch side should be about the same as the top and hinge-side gaps. Adjust by moving the jamb with your hand and inserting shims. Nail the jamb in place. Open and close the door to check that it clears the jamb by a consistent $\frac{1}{8}$ inch. Set by driving 8d finishing nails every 16 inches through the latch-side casing. Tack the door stops in position and check them by closing the door. Attach the stops.

Remove the center screw from the top hinge leaf and replace it with one long enough to penetrate into the

framing. This will help prevent the door from sagging and binding.

Install the casing on both sides of the door. Mount the door hardware.

BEFORE YOU INSTALL

Make sure the door opens in the right direction.

Test-fit the lockset. Holes bored too small can be redrilled. Holes that are too large will have to be plugged, sanded, and rebored. It is easier to return a prehung door for a different one rather than attempting to make a hole smaller. If all else fails, see if a woodwork shop will do this.

YOU'LL NEED

TIME: 2 hours to install a prehung unit in a rough opening.

SKILLS: Nailing, leveling, shimming.

TOOLS: Hammer, level, framing square, plumb bob, tape measure or ruler, saw or utility knife.

DOOR TRIM IDEAS

The most basic trim helps define and spruce up wall surfaces. The most popular style of trim for many homes today is the stock colonial-style casing. But that's only one option. Wider trim with flutes, corner blocks, and other features adds architectural quality and definition, making walls more fashionable. The variety of trim available allows you to tie together different types and sizes of room entries. Trim enables you to add the illusion of height and scale to front entries. Decorative headers and fluted casings help you set your front entry apart from the sameness of neighboring houses.

FRAME BOLD WALL COLOR
Trimming door arches with bright white molding frames the bold wall colors of each room in this home. The crown and base moldings provide additional anchors for the primary colors adorning the walls.

CREATE TRANSITIONS
Decorative trim around the door between this enclosed porch and dining room helps to visually tie together the two spaces as the door trim coordinates with the crown molding and shelves in the dining room.

INSTALL A CUSTOM LOOK
The trim on the interior door between this kitchen and pantry echoes the trim elsewhere in the rooms. Repeating a subtle architectural detail such as this provides decorative impact.

BUILDING A WALL

Behind most finished residential walls lies a rather simple construction. Vertical members, called studs, butt at the top and bottom against horizontal members, called plates. Although it looks straightforward, building a wall takes some planning. When you cover the framing with sheets of drywall or paneling, the seams between sheets must fall at the center of studs. In addition, nailing surfaces must be provided for the sheets at all the corners (see page 54), and all framing members must be aligned along a flat plane.

If the floor and ceiling are nearly level, it's easy to preassemble a stud wall on the floor and then raise it into position. If the floor and ceiling are uneven or if you're building the wall in tight quarters, it's best to build the wall in place, custom-cutting each stud to fit and toenailing it to the top and bottom plates (see pages 53–54).

Whichever approach you choose, make sure you have a way to attach your wall to the ceiling. If the wall runs perpendicular to the ceiling joists, simply fasten the wall's top plate with two 16d nails at every joist. If it runs parallel to the joists, you will have to install cross braces so you can nail the top plate into solid material (see page 52).

1 MARK THE WALL LOCATION.

Begin by deciding exactly where the wall will go. Use a framing square and a chalk line to mark its location on the floor. For long walls, check for square using the 3-4-5 method (see page 110).

Using a level and a straight 2×4 that is as high as your ceiling, mark the wall location on the ceiling, joists, or crossbracing. These marks will help you position the wall before you plumb it. Make sure there is adequate framing in the ceiling to which you can nail the top plate.

2 CUT AND MARK THE PLATES.

Using your floor layout as a guide, mark and cut 2×4s for the top and bottom plates (usually the same length). Place them on edge beside each other and mark for the studs. The first stud will be at the end of the wall. Put the center of the next stud 16 inches from the end of the wall.

Place remaining studs 16 inches on center (OC) so the distance from the center of one stud to the next is 16 inches. With a combination or speed square, draw lines ¾ inch on each side of your stud centers. Draw an X between the marks to show where to nail the studs.

Building a wall *(continued)*

3 PROVIDE NAILERS; CUT STUDS.

If your new wall runs parallel to the ceiling joists, cut pieces of 2× material to fit tightly between the ceiling joists and install them every 2 feet or so. Measure for your studs (see page 51) and cut them to length.

4 ASSEMBLE THE WALL.

Working on a flat surface, lay the studs on edge between the top and bottom plates. It helps to have something solid, such as a wall, to hold the framing against while you assemble and nail the wall.

5 RAISE THE FRAME.

Framework can be cumbersome, so have a helper on hand. Position the bottom plate about where it needs to go and tip the wall into position. If the wall fits so tightly against the ceiling that you have to hammer it into place, protect the framing with a scrap of 2×4 as you pound. Tap both ends of the frame until it is roughly plumb in both directions.

6 SNUG THE FRAME WITH SHIMS.

If the wall is a bit short in places, drive shims between the bottom plate and the floor or between the top plate and the ceiling joists. Shimming the top is best. Have your helper steady the framework while you drive the pieces into place. Drive shims from both sides, thin edge to thin edge, to keep the plate from tilting.

7 FASTEN FRAME TO WALL AND FLOOR.

After the frame is snug, recheck that the wall is plumb in both directions. Check both ends of the wall and every other stud. Fasten the top plate to the ceiling by driving a 16d nail through the plate and into each joist or nailer. Fasten the bottom plate to the floor. Use 16d nails if the floor is wood; use masonry nails or a power hammer if the floor is concrete.

GETTING THE STUD LENGTH CORRECT

Few things are more frustrating than building a stud wall only to find that your measurements were off and the wall is ¼ inch too tall. When that happens, the only thing you can do is take the wall down, pull off one plate, remove the nails, cut all the studs, and nail the wall back together again.

To measure for stud length, nail together two scraps of 2×4 to represent the top and bottom plates. Set this double 2×4 on the floor, measure up to the joist, and subtract ¼ inch for shimming. Take measurements every few feet.

BUILDING A WALL IN PLACE

If building a wall on the floor and raising it into position is not practical in your situation, construct the wall in place.

Walls are typically built with 2×4 framing lumber. Existing or new plumbing may require more space than provided in a standard wall. Use 2×6 framing lumber to build a wall that will contain large plumbing such as waste standpipes. You will need to use metal straps to join the framing members when wall plates are placed to fit pipes or mechanical fixtures joining them together.

If you want to insulate against sound, build a wall with 2×6 top and bottom plates and staggered 2×4 studs. Weave fiberglass insulation between the studs to establish a barrier that reduces din and provides a quiet sanctuary. Add soundproof drywall for an additional barrier.

Before finishing the wall with drywall, have the local building inspector check the construction. The inspector will want to make sure that plumbing and wiring are properly installed, so have them in place and exposed for review. Few things are more time-consuming, expensive, and frustrating than having to remove drywall so the building inspector can check the work.

1 INSTALL TOP AND BOTTOM PLATES.

Cut the top and bottom plates and mark them for stud locations (see page 51). Transfer the marks to the faces of the plates, making sure the marks are clear so you can see them easily to align the studs while toenailing.

If the ceiling is unfinished, finding the joists will be easy. If the ceiling is finished, you will need to locate them. Use a stud finder to locate the first joist. Mark both sides of the joist. The rest of the joists should be on 16-inch centers, so you can measure to locate them, but double-check the location with the stud finder.

Nail the top plate to the joists. Use a level and a straight board to mark the location of the bottom plate or use a chalk line case as a plumb bob. Mark the floor in two places and make an X to indicate on which side of the mark the plate should be positioned. Use masonry nails or a power hammer to fasten the bottom plate to the floor.

YOU'LL NEED

TIME: About 4 to 5 hours depending on the size of the wall.

SKILLS: Measuring, leveling, and plumbing; drilling and driving screws; shimming.

TOOLS: Tape measure, level, framing square, hammer.

SOUNDPROOF YOUR WALL

Install fiberglass insulation to dampen the noise from room to room:

Install top and bottom plates that are wider than the studs. Stagger the placement of the studs flush to opposite sides of the top and base plates.

Purchase fiberglass insulation in batts or rolls and weave it between the studs along the length of the wall. Fill to the full height of the studs.

Attach soundproof drywall to both sides of the wall for added dampening. Finish by covering with regular drywall.

Building a wall in place *(continued)*

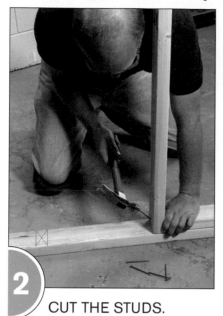

2 CUT THE STUDS.

With top and bottom plates installed, measure the required length of each stud individually. Add 1/16 inch for a snug fit and cut. Tap each stud into place. If you really have to whack it to get it into place, it is too long. Don't risk splitting the stud; take it down and trim it a little.

3 TOENAIL THE STUDS.

To secure the studs, drive 8d nails at an angle through the side of studs and into the plate; this is called toenailing. Tap the nail once or twice while holding it parallel to the floor or ceiling. When the nail tip bites into the wood, change the angle to 45 degrees. Drive four to six nails into each joint, two on each side, with an optional one at the front and back. The first nail may move the stud, but the second nail, driven from the other side, will move it back.

If you have difficulty toenailing, drill pilot holes for the nails using a 3/32-inch bit. Or place a 14½-inch board between studs to serve as a temporary nailing brace.

4 FRAME AT CORNERS.

When framing corners, make sure there is a nailing surface for every piece of drywall or paneling that will be installed. This means adding nonstructural nailers.

In Situation 1, *right,* the extra stud is turned sideways to offer a nailing surface and strengthen the corner. Drive 16d nails first through end stud #1 and into the extra stud, then through end stud #2 and into the extra stud and end stud #1.

In Situation 2, *right,* several foot-long 2×4 scraps (usually three in a standard 8-foot wall) serve as spacers between two full-length studs placed at the end of one wall. Tie the wall sections together with 16d nails. Situation 3, *right,* shows two intersecting walls. Nail three studs together and to the plates, then attach to the adjoining wall.

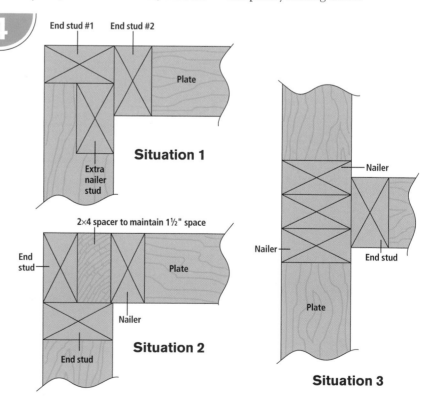

End stud #1 End stud #2

Plate

Situation 1

Extra nailer stud

2×4 spacer to maintain 1½" space

End stud

Plate

Nailer

Situation 2

End stud

Nailer

Nailer

End stud

Plate

Situation 3

If you plan to install a door in your wall, find out the rough opening dimensions you'll need. For a prehung door, measure the outside dimensions of the jamb and add ½ inch for shimming. With a slab door (one that is not prehung), measure the width of the door, add 2½ inches for the side jambs and shims, and add 2 inches to the height for the head jamb, shims, and flooring. Standard door widths are 24, 26, 28, 30, 32, and 36 inches. Door heights usually are 80 inches.

Once you know the opening's size, build the wall as described on pages 51–54, with the addition of the framing members shown below. Each has a special function.

Jack studs are the vertical 2×4s on each side of the door opening. They are attached to a king stud or to another jack stud. This doubling of studs provides solid, unbending support for the door.

The header is made of two 2×6s with a ½-inch plywood spacer sandwiched in between. (The plywood is needed to make the header 3½ inches thick, the same thickness as the wall framing.) The header rests on top of the jack studs and spans the top of the opening, supporting overhead loads. For openings that are less than 3 feet wide, you can use 2×4s instead of 2×6s.

Cripples are the short 2×4s added between the header and the top plate. They maintain a 16-inch on-center stud spacing for nailing drywall and help distribute the weight equally.

A window opening is like a door opening. You install a sill at the bottom of the window and add cripples between it and the wall's bottom plate.

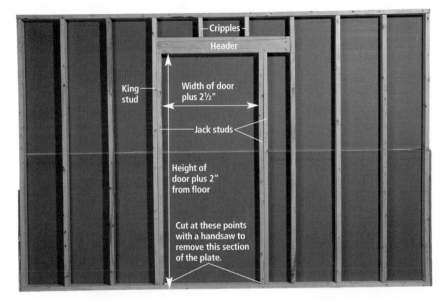

Cripples

Header

King stud

Width of door plus 2½"

Jack studs

Height of door plus 2" from floor

Cut at these points with a handsaw to remove this section of the plate.

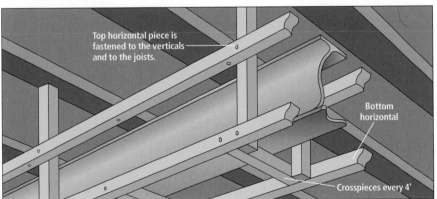

Top horizontal piece is fastened to the verticals and to the joists.

Bottom horizontal

Crosspieces every 4'

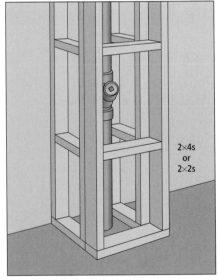

2×4s or 2×2s

FRAME AROUND AN I-BEAM.

Use 2×2s to frame around a narrow obstruction, such as a beam. Fasten the frame together with screws rather than nails because the structure will be wobbly as you work. Drill pilot holes whenever you drive a screw near the end of a board. Make chalk lines on the joists 1⅝ inches out from either side of the beam. On every other joist, attach a vertical 2×2, cutting it to extend 1¾ inches below the bottom of the beam. Fasten horizontal pieces to the bottom ends of the verticals, then fasten horizontal pieces at the top, driving screws into both the vertical supports and the joists. Finish the framing by installing horizontal crosspieces about every 4 feet between the bottom horizontal frame members.

FRAME AROUND A PIPE.

You can cover a soil stack or other tall, narrow obstruction with a frame. Mark lines on the floor and measure for top and bottom plates as you would for a regular wall. Draw plumb lines on the wall to use as guides. Build three narrow walls of 2×4s or 2×2s; raise them into position; and fasten them to the floor, ceiling, wall, and each other.

WALL FRAME IDEAS

Wall frames provide an architectural flair to a room well within the reach of the average do-it-yourself homeowner. Easier to install than wainscoting, wall frames can be as simple as a series of frames creating a raised pattern of trimwork on a wall. Or custom tailor the frames to fit a variety of room designs. Create enclosures of surfaces. Provide an illusion of three dimensions to walls with varying richness, substance, and depth.

Wall frames originate from the Georgian period of the mid-1700s. During that time, plaster replaced wooden wall panels as the predominate décor. The elegant accents of wall frames helped popularize the use of color schemes. Frames create the illusion of enhanced visual space while dividing walls into aesthetically pleasing spaces.

> **VARY SIZES**
> Keep an eye for scale. In a well-designed room, the base molding may be wider than the chair rail, the chair rail more massive than the door and window casing, and the wall frames the lightest element.

> **ACHIEVE A DRAMATIC RESULT**
> Wall frames give impact and dramatic emphasis to the lower wall.

CREATE A PLEASING EFFECT

The structure, progression, and relation of wall frames create a pleasing architectural whole blending diversity and unity. The diversity of the intersecting vertical and horizontal lines of the room are emphasized by the linear aspects of the frames, while the progression and repetition produce a unity of design.

CONSIDER THE OVERALL LOOK

A satisfying arrangement of proportional frames balances a wall. Experiment with the frames. All do not have to be the same size. If you have space for only three frames in your design, make the middle frame wider. With five frames, balance the wall by making the middle and end frames narrower.

REPEAT PATTERNS

Repetition suggests movement as the eye follows and anticipates a pattern. The repetition of frames throughout a space generates a rhythm unique to the room.

Wall frame ideas *(continued)*

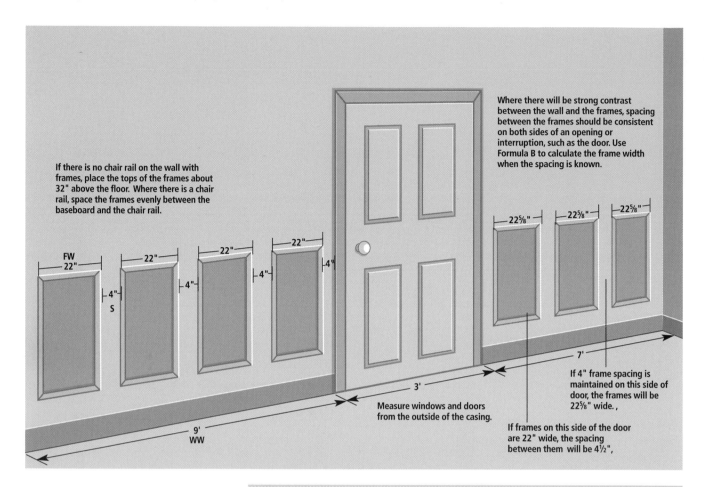

If there is no chair rail on the wall with frames, place the tops of the frames about 32" above the floor. Where there is a chair rail, space the frames evenly between the baseboard and the chair rail.

FW 22"

S

22"

4"

22"

4"

22"

4"

22"

4"

4"

Where there will be strong contrast between the wall and the frames, spacing between the frames should be consistent on both sides of an opening or interruption, such as the door. Use Formula B to calculate the frame width when the spacing is known.

22⅝" 22⅝" 22⅝"

7'

3'

Measure windows and doors from the outside of the casing.

9'
WW

If 4" frame spacing is maintained on this side of door, the frames will be 22⅝" wide.

If frames on this side of the door are 22" wide, the spacing between them will be 4½".

LAYING OUT THE WALL.

Measure the wall and its doors and windows. Sketch the wall, then determine how many frames you want. A frame below a window should be the same width as the window. Estimate the length of each frame, then use Formula A in the box at the right to calculate the spacing. Adjust the frame length and spacing for the most pleasing effect.

On the wall shown, the spacing works out differently for the panels on each side of the door. You can vary either the frame width or the spacing to fit the frames onto the wall. In this case, it's probably better to keep the spacing consistent along the wall by changing the size of the three panels on the 7-foot wall, using Formula B at right. Adding ⅝" to the frame width will be less noteceable than adding ½" to the 4" spacing between the frames.

FRAME SPACING

Formula A. This formula calculates the spacing between frames when the frame width is known. Decide how many frames will fit on the wall, then calculate the space between the frames and at each end of the array (S) using the formula below. Express all measurements in the same unit.

$$S = \{WW - (FW \times F)\} \div (F+1)$$

WW=Width of wall
FW=Width of one frame
F=Number of frames

Example:
WW=9' (108"), FW=22", F=4

$S = \{108" - 88"\} \div 5$
$S = 20" \div 5$
$S = 4"$

Formula B . This formula calculates the frame width when spacing between the frames is known. Determine how many frames will fit on the wall, then calculate the frame width (FW) using the formula below. Be sure to express all measurements in the same unit.

$$FW = \{WW - S \times (F+1)\} \div F.$$

WW=Width of wall
S=Space between frames
F=Number of frames

Example:
WW=7'(84"), S=4", F=3

$FW = 84" - (4" \times 4) \div 3$
$FW = 68" \div 3;$
$FW = 22⅝"$ approximately

INSTALLING WALL FRAMES

Emphasize your walls. Wall frames dress up any room. They are three-dimensional and divide the wall area into smaller geometric, dense spaces.

The possibilities and combinations are unlimited. Design with a motif in mind. Wall frames create drama by enhancing the dynamics of a wall. They grab the eye and direct your attention.

Create a rhythm by having a wide wall frame flanked by narrower frames in a progression. The arrangement of proportional frames gives balance to a wall. Experiment with frames. They do not all need to be the same size. If you have space for only three frames in your design, make the middle frame wider. Balance a wall using five frames by making the middle and end frames narrower.

Keep an eye on scale. A well-designed room might include a base molding wider than the chair rail, the chair rail more massive than the door and window casing, and the wall frames providing a delicate accent.

YOU'LL NEED

TIME: About 1 day, longer if you need to address awkard situations.

SKILLS: Cutting, measuring, gluing, fastening with nails, sanding, painting, staining.

TOOLS: Tape measure, chalk line, pencil, framing square, saw, speed or combination square, level, power drill with screwdriver bit, scrap plywood, nail set, wood filler, hammer.

1 MAKE A TEMPLATE.

Constructing a template makes easy work of building wall frames. Attach a square piece of plywood the inside dimensions of the frame to a larger piece of plywood. The plywood should be at least ½ inch thick, allowing you to apply pressure for gluing mitered edges to create a tight joint. The bottom piece should extend 1½ inches beyond the smaller piece to provide a solid base.

2 GLUE THE ENDS.

Assemble the miter-cut pieces around the inner piece of plywood, gluing the mitered ends. Fasten with an air nailer or use a hammer with finishing nails. Prevent the frame ends from splitting by predrilling the holes. Drive the nailheads below the surface with a nail set.

3 SNAP A CHALK LINE.

Measure from the bottom of the chair rail to the top of the wall frame at opposite ends of the wall.

Stretch a chalk line between the points and snap it for a guideline.

Installing wall frames (continued)

4 MARK MOLDING PLACEMENT.

Mark the top corners of each wall frame on the chalk line. Make two guides from scraps: one the interval width between frames and one the width to the chair rail.

5 LEVEL THE FRAME.

Apply adhesive to the back of the first frame and position it on the wall using the chalk line and your guides. Check for level. Adjust.

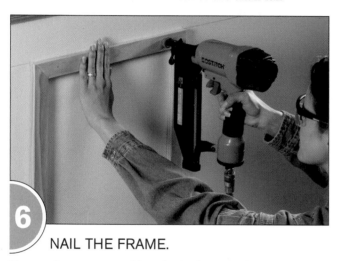

6 NAIL THE FRAME.

Fasten the top using 6d nails. Make sure the frame is plumb and level.

7 SECURE THE SIDES AND BOTTOM.

Fasten the sides then bottom of the frame. Set the nails below the wood surface.

8 APPLY WOOD FILLER.

Fill the holes with wood filler. Caulk the gaps on the inside and outside. Allow to dry.

9 FINISH THE SURFACE.

Sand to finish (see pages 151–152). Prime and paint, or stain and seal.

PLANNING FOR A CHAIR RAIL

Chair rail molding protects the wall from chairs, but this is only one of the uses of this versatile style of molding. Use it as casing, base, wallpaper border, or panel molding. Installing a chair rail will create a dramatic addition to any room.

A chair rail in its basic sense is a piece of molding that runs around your room's perimeter a little less than halfway up the wall. To be exact, it is typically positioned 32 inches above the floor. Many people like to dress the walls above and below the chair rail. For example, you may wish to paint the sections of the wall different colors or wallpaper one section and paint the other. You may also paint or stain the chair rail the same color as or a different color from the background wall.

<

DIVIDE A WALL FOR DRAMA
A chair rail like this one suggests painting the wall in two colors. After you have completed the steps for installing a chair rail on page 63, consider the color scheme you want to use. For a subtle look, choose two shades of the same color. For a more dramatic look, use a light and a dark color. Paint the darker shade below the chair rail to visually anchor the space.

>

DISPLAY ART
Create a picture rail like this one by adding a wide top cap to a crown molding placed at chair-rail height. Pictures can easily be repositioned along the molding to accommodate a changing collection.

Planning for a chair rail *(continued)*

Plate rail

Chair rail

> **CRAFT A LEDGE FOR PLATES**
Put a twist on a traditional chair rail and create a plate rail for displaying a plate collection. Follow the steps for installing a chair rail on page 63, but select molding wide enough for your collection. To secure plates, see page 126 for router techniques to make a groove the length of the molding.

INSTALLING A CHAIR RAIL

Traditionally chair rails protected walls from chairs. Wallcoverings above the chair rail stayed clean, while the painted area below the molding could be washed, repaired, or repainted to hide wear and tear. Today chair rails are more decorative, used in traditional and colonial decor. Chair rails afford a number of decorating options. The wall below the chair rail can be painted much darker than the area above for dramatic contrast. Subtle differences in color can be applied above and below the rail for a much softer overall look. You can build a custom chair rail, as shown here, or install stock chair rail moldings.

1 SNAP A CHALK LINE.

Establish the height of the chair rail. Mark the height at a couple of locations along each wall. Stretch a chalk line along the marks. Check for level. Snap the chalk line to establish a guideline.

2 LEVEL THE WALL TRIM.

Align the wall trim piece along the line. Have a helper hold the piece in place and make sure the trim is level. Use a hammer and finishing nails or a pneumatic finishing nailer to attach the trim to the wall.

3 MARK FOR THE CAP.

Set a cap on top of the trim. Butt against the door casing and mark a line on the end of the cap parallel to the casing. This establishes the start location for cutting a 45-degree angle on the cap.

4 GLUE THE RAIL.

Apply a generous amount of wood glue along the top of the main rail. This will provide additional strength for the cap.

5 NAIL THE CAP.

Fasten the cap rail to the main rail using finishing nails.

6 SAND THE RAIL.

Finish the chair rail with cap, main rail, and cove molding below the cap and cove molding below the main rail. Set all nails below the surface. Fill the holes with wood filler, let dry, and sand to finish. Prime and paint, or stain and seal.

YOU'LL NEED

TIME: 3 to 4 hours.

SKILLS: Cutting, measuring, gluing, fastening with nails, sanding, painting, staining.

TOOLS: Tape measure, chalk line, pencil, framing square, saw, speed or combination square, level, miter box or mitersaw, nail set, wood filler, hammer.

PLANNING FOR A WINDOW

If quick-fix repairs to your windows aren't doing the job, it's time to consider putting in replacements. Because most window replacements may require a custom window, allow six to eight weeks for delivery. You will need to plan this project ahead.

Always replace an exterior window damaged by severe weather or that has warped. Windows that need constant repair or adjustment are candidates for replacement. A new, energy-efficient window keeps cold drafts out of your home and saves you dollars in the long run. Double- or triple-paned thermal windows allow far less heat to escape your home in the winter and less heat in during the summer, lowering your fuel bills considerably. You can expect a drop of 20 to 30 percent when you replace with energy-efficient windows.

When replacing a window, start by removing the trim. Use a flat pry bar to carefully pry away the trim so as not to damage the exterior and interior of your home. If you have an old double-hung window with sash weights, remove the weights by cutting the cords and pulling the weights out of their pockets. To remove the old window casing, remove the nails holding it in place. It may be easier to use a reciprocating saw to cut the nails rather than pulling them with a hammer claw. If the window casing has nailing fins, remove a portion of the siding to pull the mounting nails. Have a helper assist you with pulling the window out of the rough opening using a pry bar.

>

MANY WINDOWS MAKE A BRIGHT BATHROOM
Adding a bank of windows to a room such as this bathroom brings an abundance of sunlight and scenery. When planning windows for bathrooms, consider whether privacy needs will require window treatments.

‹

PLAN A PLACE FOR A WINDOW
For a new window installation, such as in this home office, consider how you will use and arrange the room before finalizing window placement. In this case, the window was positioned just above the desktop to flood it with natural light and to provide a pleasant view while working.

‹

MEASURE CAREFULLY
Taking accurate measurements of a wall of windows requires special care. Measure the width of a window from outside trim edge to outside trim edge. Before finalizing your window replacement plans, measure twice to ensure accuracy.

INSTALLING A WINDOW

Before you buy a replacement for an old window, think about the style and size of the new window. Consider the window's location and whether you want a smaller or larger replacement. Don't assume that you must replace your old window with an exact duplicate.

SHOPPING TIPS

Look for the National Fenestration Rating Council (NFRC) label. It states the window you purchased meets council standards.

Remember, the lower the U-value, the better the insulation factor. A U-value of 0.35 or below is recommended for cold climates. The window should have at least double glazing and low-E coating.

Where the summertime heat is a concern, look for windows with double glazing and spectrally selective coatings. These windows will reduce heat gain.

Select windows with air leakage ratings of 0.3 cubic feet per minute or less.

Look for the Energy Star and Energy Guide labels.

YOU'LL NEED

TIME: 3 to 4 hours per window.

SKILLS: Layout, measuring, cutting, and hammering.

TOOLS: Hammer, reciprocating saw, caulking gun, circular saw, tape measure, level, drill.

1 ADD FRAMING.

Not all replacement windows are the same size as the original windows. Add framing to the opening if the new window is smaller. Make sure the window opening is plumb and level.

2 TEST-FIT THE WINDOW.

Have a helper assist you with placing the window in the center of the opening. Support the window with wooden blocks or shims.

3 CHECK FOR LEVEL.

Make sure that the window is level and plumb. Adjust with shims and blocking.

4 TACK IN PLACE.

If the window has nailing fins, drive 2-inch roofing nails through the holes. Leave the nailheads exposed so you can remove the nails if you encounter problems during the installation.

5 CHECK FOR PLUMB.

If the window was square when it was set and the sill was level, the jamb should be plumb. Check again for plumb. Adjust by placing shims between the jamb and framing. Open and close the window to make sure it operates smoothly. Fasten the window in place.

6 INSULATE AROUND THE WINDOW.

Insulation saves on heating bills by preventing outside air from entering. Push the insulation into the gap, but don't pack it tightly. Always wear gloves, protective eyewear, and a dust mask when handling fiberglass insulation.

7 ATTACH THE EXTERIOR CASING.

Fasten the casing while checking the head jamb for level and the side jambs for plumb. Drive nails or screws on 12-inch centers. Caulk the gap between the window casing and the siding as well as underneath the sill. Use a quality exterior caulk. Attach the window's interior casing.

8 FINISH THE INTERIOR.

Install trimwork as the final step. Full trimwork for a window includes the stool, apron, and window casing. You will need to choose whether to install stain-grade or paint-grade trim. You also will need to decide on the type of wood. Drive the interior nails and install the interior trim. Caulk the perimeter of the window.

WORKING WITH METAL STUDS

Metal framing costs a good deal less than wood 2×4s, and it is lighter. Metal is not susceptible to rot or insect damage, and the factory-made pieces are free from bows, twists, knots, and other imperfections that sometimes make wood hard to work with.

Working with metal studs takes some adjustments. You can't build walls on the floor then raise them up. Instead, you must install the top and floor runners, then insert the studs. Cut metal studs with tin snips or a circular saw fitted with a metal-cutting blade. Fasten the pieces together with self-tapping screws.

If you make a mistake, it usually is easier to move a metal stud than a wood one. Electrical wiring and pipes for plumbing are easy to run through precut punch-out holes in the studs.

On the downside, once walls are built, you can't attach items to metal stud walls as easily as you can to wood walls. You can fasten items to a metal stud with a screw but not a nail. If you plan to hang cabinets or shelves on the wall, crossbrace the wall with C-runners or 2×4 blocking. Door jambs and windows can be attached to steel framing, but it's easier to shim and attach the units if you use wood framing, fastened to the metal studs, around these openings.

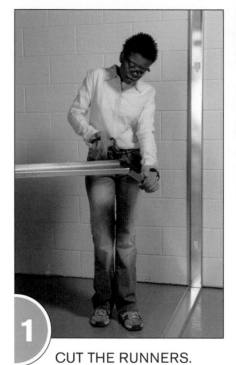

1 CUT THE RUNNERS.

Lay out the framing as you would for a wood wall (see pages 53–54). With tin snips, cut the runners to be used for top and bottom plates to length. Or use a metal-cutting blade on a circular saw. A circular saw is faster, but throws metal filings. Make sure no one is in the area as you cut and wear protective eyewear and clothing as you work.

2 ATTACH THE CEILING RUNNER.

Position the ceiling runner and attach it to each joist with a 2-inch drywall screw. If joists run parallel to the wall, install crossmembers, to which you can attach the runner. Using a plumb bob, position the floor runner directly below the ceiling runner. Attach it to the floor with screws or masonry nails.

YOU'LL NEED

TIME: 1 to 2 hours to build a basic 12-foot wall.

SKILLS: Measuring and marking for walls, cutting with tin snips, fastening with a drill or screw gun.

TOOLS: Tape measure, level, tin snips or circular saw with metal-cutting blade, chalk line, drill or screw gun, plumb bob.

CAUTION

METAL STUDS ARE SHARP

The ends of metal studs, especially those that you cut, often are very sharp. When working with metal, wear gloves. If you're cutting with a circular saw and metal-cutting blade, wear long sleeves that are not loose or floppy.

Cutting metal also can be dangerous because small pieces of metal fly through the air. Be sure to wear eye protection whenever you cut metal studs.

If you run electrical wiring through metal framing, use sections of plastic foam pipe insulation or specially made plastic grommets to protect wires from damage.

3 CUT AND INSERT THE STUDS.

Cut the studs to length with tin snips. Insert them into the runners, starting at a slight angle and twisting them into place. For easier plumbing or electrical installation, make sure all the stud legs point in the same direction and all the predrilled punch-outs line up.

4 ATTACH STUDS TO THE RUNNERS.

Once studs are placed correctly, drive $7/16$-inch pan- or wafer-head screws through the runners into the studs. Hold the stud flange firmly against the runner as you work. Drive four screws, one on either side of each runner at the top and bottom.

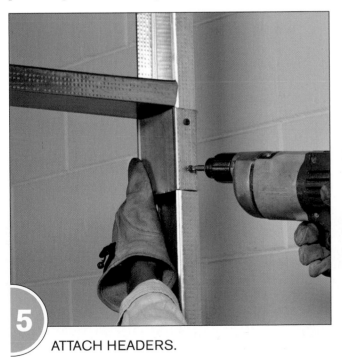

5 ATTACH HEADERS.

Where you need a door or window header, cut a piece of runner 8 inches longer than the width of the opening. Cut the two sides of the runner 4 inches from each end so you can bend back a tab, as shown. Slip the tabs into place and attach with screws.

6 INSTALL THE DRYWALL.

Inspect the framing to make sure you have a fastening surface for drywall at all points. Attach the drywall with drywall screws placed 8 to 12 inches apart. Install corner beads with screws or staples. Tape and finish the walls (see pages 76–77).

FURRING BASEMENT WALLS

When finishing basement walls, you can build stud walls (see pages 51–54), and fasten them to the concrete or masonry walls. A stud wall goes up quickly, gives you room to add plenty of insulation, and ensures that the new walls will be straight, even if the existing walls are not. However, you lose some floor space because of the thickness of the walls.

If insulation is not a problem and your basement walls are smooth and straight, you can save money in materials and preserve some square footage by fastening 1×2, 1×3, or 1×4 furring strips to the walls.

The layout is the same as it is for stud walls. The ends of drywall or paneling sheets and all joints must fall on a furring strip, and there must be nailing surfaces at all corners.

The construction method, however, is different. Furring strips are individually attached to the wall, shimmed where necessary, with glue and masonry nails or with a power hammer, which shoots nails with gunpowder charges (see page 71).

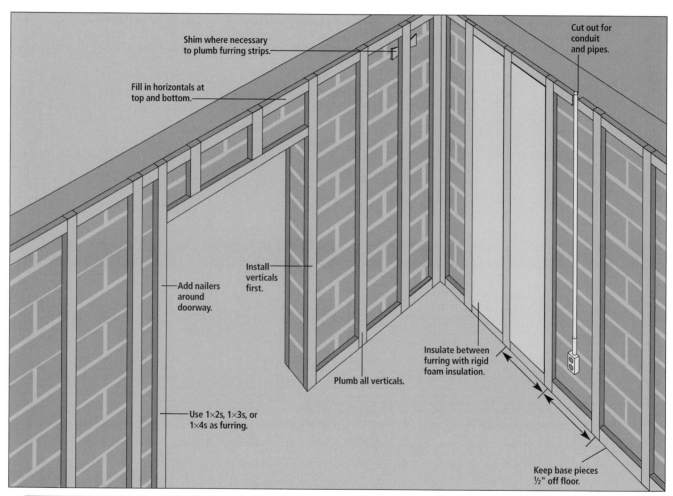

Shim where necessary to plumb furring strips.

Fill in horizontals at top and bottom.

Cut out for conduit and pipes.

Add nailers around doorway.

Install verticals first.

Plumb all verticals.

Insulate between furring with rigid foam insulation.

Use 1×2s, 1×3s, or 1×4s as furring.

Keep base pieces ½" off floor.

YOU'LL NEED

TIME: 1 day for a 12×12-foot room.

SKILLS: Laying out, measuring, cutting, hammering.

TOOLS: Hammer, baby sledge, caulking gun, circular saw, tape measure, level, chalk line.

PLAN THE FURRING LAYOUT.

Begin the job by marking the locations of the vertical furring strips. One easy way to do this is to position a sheet of your wall material in the corner of the room, plumb it, and strike a chalk line down its outside edge to mark the centerline for one strip. Using this line as a guide and 16 inches as the center-to-center measurement, mark the locations of the other vertical strips along that wall.

Measure and cut each strip to fit between the floor and ceiling. Cut each piece ½ inch short so that it will be fastened a bit above the floor as a safeguard against moisture.

1 APPLY ADHESIVE.

With a caulking gun, squeeze a wavy ¼-inch bead of construction adhesive onto the furring strip. As you finish, release the pressure on the adhesive, discontinuing the flow. Push the strip against the wall in its correct location, pressing firmly to help spread the adhesive.

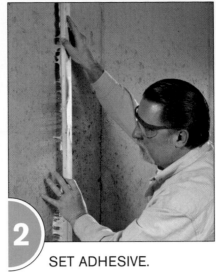

2 SET ADHESIVE.

Pull the strip off the wall and lean it against another wall to let the adhesive begin to set up. After letting it set for the time specified by the manufacturer, press the strip back into place.

3 PLUMB AND SHIM.

Check the strip for plumb. If a dip or bulge is noticeable to the eye, tuck pairs of shims behind the strip and wedge it into line. Double-check your work as the job progresses by holding a straightedge horizontally across four or five vertical pieces. Correct any gaps or bulges.

4 DRIVE IN FASTENERS.

Hammer concrete nails through the strip and the shims and into the masonry wall. On a brick or block wall, it often is easiest to drive the nails into the mortar joints. Use a baby sledge if you have one. Driving nails into concrete walls is extremely difficult; consider a power hammer (see "Tools to Use," *right*).

5 ADD THE HORIZONTALS.

After all the verticals are in place, aligned, and secured, begin work on the top and bottom horizontal pieces. Measure and cut them one at a time. Apply adhesive, shim if necessary, and install them as you installed the verticals.

TOOLS TO USE

Power hammer. Choose a power hammer that loads quickly. It usually makes sense to rent a better quality power tool rather than to buy a cheap one. Experiment with several types of loads to find one powerful enough to drive the nails in, but not so powerful as to drive them completely through the furring strips. Note: Follow the manufacturer's directions carefully. A power hammer is closely related to firearms and is dangerous if misused.

Quart-size caulking gun. On large jobs, this tool will pay for itself because adhesive purchased in large tubes costs less per ounce. It also will save you time and create less mess because you'll need to change tubes only once for each 2½ of the smaller tubes.

Drywall is inexpensive, and any homeowner has the skills needed to hang and finish it. But hanging drywall is difficult work. The sheets are heavy and unwieldy. Making cutouts for electrical boxes and pipes can be tedious. Careful installation makes finishing easier.

Finishing drywall to a smooth surface takes three applications of compound and sandings for professionals—perhaps more for beginners. Some homeowners prefer to have a professional install and finish drywall.

Check framing to make sure you have adequate nailing surfaces (see page 74). Add framing members where you need them. If you are covering an existing wall, locate the joists and studs and clearly mark their locations on the walls and ceiling. A helper is essential—hanging drywall alone is nearly impossible.

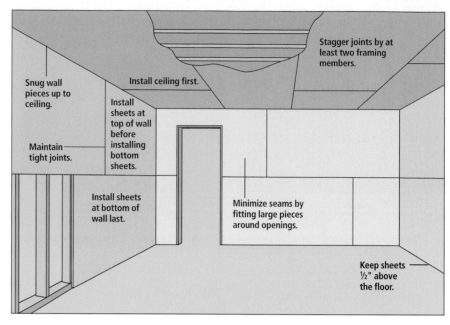

Labels on figure:
- Snug wall pieces up to ceiling.
- Install ceiling first.
- Stagger joints by at least two framing members.
- Install sheets at top of wall before installing bottom sheets.
- Maintain tight joints.
- Install sheets at bottom of wall last.
- Minimize seams by fitting large pieces around openings.
- Keep sheets ½" above the floor.

LAY OUT THE JOB.

Store drywall sheets flat or on edge on pieces of 1× or 2× scrap lumber to hold the sheets off the floor. Before cutting a sheet, make sure the finished surface is facing you.

DRYWALL SQUARE

Don't hesitate to spend the money for a drywall square (see page 84). It quickly pays for itself in time and labor savings. For crosscuts, you simply make one measurement, set the square in place, and run your knife along the square's blade for a square cut. It also simplifies rip cuts (see page 73).

YOU'LL NEED

TIME: With a helper, 1 day for a 12×12-foot room.

SKILLS: Measuring, physical strength, thoroughness.

TOOLS: Tape measure, drywall square, utility knife, drywall saw, chalk line.

1 MAKE A CROSSCUT.

Mark your cut line, stand the sheet on edge, and set your drywall square in place. Clasp the square firmly on top and brace it at its base with your foot. With the edge of the knife blade against the square, cut downward most of the way, then finish by cutting up from the bottom.

2 SNAP TO CUT.

Snap the segment back away from your cut line. Finally slice through the backing paper with your knife.

3 MEASURE FOR THE LAST PIECE.

To determine the correct cutoff length of a corner sheet, measure the distance from the last sheet to the corner at both the top and the bottom. If it is more than ¼ inch out of square, mark both ends of the cut rather than make a square cut using a drywall square.

4 MAKE A RIP CUT.

If you need to make a parallel rip cut—one that is the same width all along its length—use your drywall square. Set the square on the edge of the sheet and hold the knife against it at the measured distance. Slide the square along with the knife, cutting as you go.

MAKE A FREEHAND CUT.

Often a rip cut will not be square; it will be shorter at one end than the other. In this case, make a mark at each end of the sheet and chalk a line between the marks. Cut freehand or use a straightedge as a guide if you need precision.

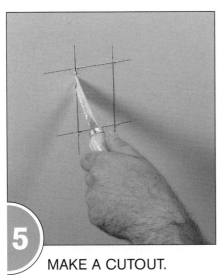

5 MAKE A CUTOUT.

To make a cutout for an electrical box, measure from the box edges to the edge of the last panel. Measure from the top and bottom of the box to the bottom of the sheet of drywall above it or the ceiling. Transfer the measurements to the sheet and draw a rectangle. Score the surface with a utility knife, then cut it with a drywall saw.

6 CUT AROUND PIPES.

To cut a hole for a pipe, measure and mark the sheet for the center of the pipe. Drill a hole using a holesaw bit that is slightly larger than the pipe diameter. Or draw a circle and cut it out with a drywall saw or a knife.

AVOID MOISTURE DAMAGE IN A BASEMENT

Wood framing can withstand occasional wetness as long as it is allowed to dry out, but drywall that gets wet once will lose its strength and crumble.

When you are drywalling a basement or another place that is subject to chronic dampness or occasional flooding, add nailers to the base of the framing and cut the drywall sheets so they are held off the floor 2 to 3 inches. When you install the baseboard molding, add furring to fill the gap.

If your basement is subject to more drastic flooding, raise the drywall even higher. To do this, install a 1×6 baseboard directly on the framing and set the drywall on top of it. This will keep the drywall 5½ inches above the floor.

HANGING DRYWALL

Be prepared for strenuous labor when you hang drywall. The sheets are heavy, you'll often have to work in awkward positions, and you'll have to hold the sheets in place while you drive nails or screws. It's tempting to rush the job, but sloppy installation makes finishing more difficult. Wide gaps between drywall sheets take a long time to tape, and nobody wants nails popping out later. Here's how to do the job correctly the first time.

ATTACH DRYWALL WITH SCREWS.

If you are using screws, the same principles apply as with nailing: The screw head must be set below the surface, but it must not break the paper. This is difficult to do with a simple screwdriver bit. Use a dimpler bit or a drywall screwdriver (see box on opposite page). Always drive in screws perpendicular to the sheet or their heads will tear the paper.

YOU'LL NEED

TIME: 20 minutes per sheet for walls, 30 minutes per ceiling sheet.

SKILLS: A strong back, fastening in difficult circumstances.

TOOLS: Tape measure, good ladders or scaffolding, hammer or drill with drywall-type screwdriver attachment, drywall taping blades.

CEILING PATTERN:
Nails only

12"

WALL PATTERNS:
Nails only

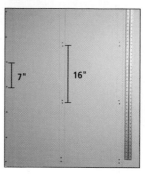

7"   16"

Nails and adhesive

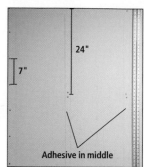

24"

7"

Adhesive in middle

NAIL OR SCREW ACCORDING TO CODE.

Local building codes specify how many nails or screws to use to hang drywall and in what sort of pattern. Codes vary not only from region to region, but from room to room; for example, more fasteners may be required in bathrooms. Check with your building department. Many professionals don't nail in pairs, but there is good reason to do so: If one nail pops through the paper, the other will hold. For ceiling panels, the general practice is to pair nails at 12-inch intervals around the perimeter and every 12 inches along each joist.

When using adhesive, install two nails at 24-inch intervals and one nail every 7 inches along the edge. Keep adhesive 6 inches away from the edges of the sheets.

Requirements are less stringent for walls. If you don't use adhesive, install two nails into the wall studs at 16-inch intervals and a single nail every 7 inches along edges.

When using adhesive, install two nails at 24-inch intervals and one nail every 7 inches along the edge. Keep adhesive 6 inches away from the top and bottom of each sheet.

WRONG: Nailhead protrudes.   **CORRECT:** Nailhead set in dimple.   **WRONG:** Paper broken.

SET NAILHEADS CORRECTLY.

If you simply drive a nail flush, you will not be able to hide it with joint compound. If you drive the nail too deeply, you will break the paper on the drywall. When the paper is broken, the nail won't hold; it tears right through the gypsum inner core. Drive the nail so the nailhead is set in a slightly dimpled surface. No portion of the nailhead should protrude above the surface of the drywall. To test if your nails are driven deeply enough, run a taping blade along the surface of the wall. You should not feel any nailheads click against the blade as you pull it across. Pull out any nails that miss a joist or stud; swat the hole with your hammer to dimple it.

INSTALL THE CEILING SHEETS.

Hang drywall on the ceiling before installing the wall sheets. Start in a corner and work out from there, keeping the panels perpendicular to the joists. Before you start take time to locate joists and mark their locations on the sheet and the wall. Searching for joists while holding the sheet up with your head is no fun. The quickest, but most difficult, way to install drywall on a ceiling is to set the panel in place and support it with your head, leaving your hands free to hold and drive nails or screws. Wearing a baseball cap greatly minimizes pulled hair and a sore head.

To make hanging drywall easier, construct one or two 2×2 T-braces to use as props. Or rent a drywall hoist (see inset). Either solution will make the process easier and result in a much neater job.

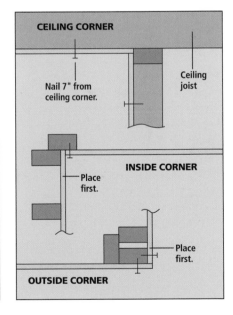

CEILING CORNER

Nail 7" from ceiling corner.

Ceiling joist

INSIDE CORNER

Place first.

Place first.

OUTSIDE CORNER

INSTALL THE WALL SHEETS.

Once the ceiling panels are up, hang sheets on the walls. If you are installing sheets horizontally, begin with the upper sheets, butting them firmly against the ceiling drywall. Make sure all vertical seams hit studs. Butt the lower panels firmly against the upper panels, tapered edge to tapered edge. Raise up sheets tightly with a wedge or lever.

If you are installing sheets vertically, check that the tapered edges fall midway across a stud. If they don't, either cut the drywall or attach pieces of lumber to the stud to give yourself a nailing surface for the next piece (see right).

Overlap pieces at corners, as shown above. Finish the job by adding the filler pieces, measuring and cutting each piece to size. Make sure each piece has at least two nailing members to support it.

TAPING DRYWALL

Once you've gained some experience, three coats of drywall compound, with sandings, will produce smooth walls. But as a beginner, don't be surprised if it takes you four or five coats. Unless you have large holes that require patching plaster, use ready-mixed drywall joint compound. Dry-mix compounds provide more strength for trouble areas, but you'll need to work fast if you use them. To hide imperfections, apply texture to your walls with a rented texture gun and hopper.

DRYWALL FINISHING TIPS

Use self-sticking mesh tape on drywall wherever a tapered edge meets a tapered edge, as shown *above right.* Use paper tape everywhere else. Mesh tape requires less joint compound but does not work as well for inside corners.

Rusty, gunked-up tools ruin your work. Scrape, wash, and dry blades after every use.

When sanding, control the fine dust by using a fan to pull it out a window. Seal doorways and wear a breathing mask.

YOU'LL NEED

TIME: For a typical bedroom, 5 hours for the first coat and 2 hours for subsequent coats, plus time for sanding and drying.

SKILLS: Patience and willingness to learn.

TOOLS: Utility knife; 6-, 10-, and 12-inch taping blades; corner taping tool; pole sander or hand sander; tin snips.

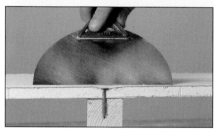

1 APPLY A BED COAT.

Conceal nailheads by putting compound on a 6-inch taping blade and passing over the spot twice. Make sure you leave compound only in the depression and not on the rest of the sheet. Do this with each coat until the dimple is filled in completely. Joints are more difficult, especially butt joints. If you are using self-sticking mesh tape, simply cut pieces to fit, press them into place, and begin applying joint compound. For paper tape, start by spreading a bed coat over the joint with a 6-inch taping blade. Apply just enough compound for the paper tape to adhere. The photo *above top* shows edges making a joint; a nail dimple is *above bottom.*

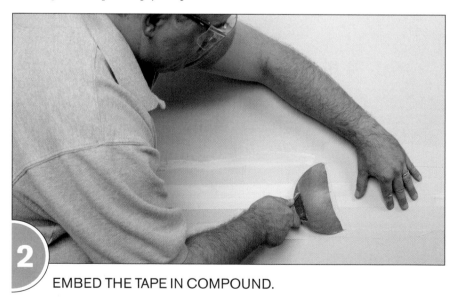

2 EMBED THE TAPE IN COMPOUND.

(Skip this step if you are using mesh tape.) Immediately after applying the bed coat to a joint, center a length of paper tape over the joint and press the tape firmly against the filled joint by running your taping blade along it. If the tape begins to slide, hold it in place with your hand. If bubbles form under the tape, if there are places where the tape is not sticking to the bed coat, or if wrinkles appear, peel the tape back and apply more compound. Then press the tape back.

APPLY COMPOUND OVER THE TAPE.

Load a 10-inch taping blade with compound and apply a smooth coat over the tape. Where two tapered edges meet, make sure the blade extends past both tapers. Fill in the tapers only so you have a flat wall surface. For butt joints, feather out the compound 7 to 9 inches on each side; a small ridge in the middle can be sanded later. After the compound dries, scrape off ridges and bumps, and sand. Apply and sand successive coats until the surface is smooth.

4 COAT OUTSIDE CORNERS.

To protect and conceal drywall edges that meet at an outside corner, cut a piece of metal corner bead using tin snips. Fit the strip over the corner and fasten it to the wall, one side at a time. Drive nails or screws at 10-inch intervals. Make sure the flange of the corner bead does not protrude above what will be the finished surface by running a taping blade along the length of the corner bead. Fasten down any areas of flange that protrude.

Apply a coat of joint compound with a 6-inch blade angled away from the corner. Allow one side of the blade to ride on the bead, the other side on the wall. For subsequent coats, use 10- and 12-inch blades.

5 TAPE INSIDE CORNERS.

Apply a bed coat of compound to both sides of an inside corner with a 6-inch blade. Cut a piece of paper tape to the correct length, fold it, and position it by hand. Keep it straight to avoid wrinkles. Run a corner taping tool along its length to embed the tape in the compound. Lift and reapply compound wherever the tape has wrinkles, bubbles, or nonadhering spots.

Once the tape is embedded, apply some compound to the walls and some to the corner tool. Stroke on a smooth coat. This will take several passes and some practice. You may find it easier to feather out the edges with a 10-inch taping blade.

INSTALLING PANELING

Sheet paneling needs a solid, plumb backing. Typically this is a stud wall covered with ½-inch drywall. On the inside of exterior and below-grade walls, sandwich insulation and a vapor barrier between the studs and the drywall to protect panels from moisture.

As you estimate materials, keep in mind that panel seams must hit studs. Lay out the job to avoid thin strips of paneling. It's better to cut 14 inches off the first panel on a wall than end up with a piece 2 inches wide at the end of the wall. Stand the panels up for 48 hours in the room in which they'll be installed to acclimate them.

CHOOSING PANELING

Sheet paneling is inexpensive and easy to install, but it is also thin and flexible. Paneling will accentuate wavy walls rather than hide them.

If you have problem walls, consider tongue-and-groove planks. They are more expensive and take longer to install, but they'll straighten the walls. Planking requires furring strips and shims every 16 vertical inches for backing.

Be sure to inspect sheet paneling for variations in color, flaws, and splinters.

YOU'LL NEED

TIME: About 1 day to panel a medium-size room.

SKILLS: Measuring, scribing, cutting sheets, nailing.

TOOLS: Level, hammer, nail set, utility knife, caulking gun, circular or jigsaw.

1 MARK THE SEAMS.

Mark the location of the studs where the panel edges will meet. Cut the first sheet so its edge falls on the middle of the stud. Set the first piece in place without nailing it. Panels should have a ¹⁄₁₆-inch gap between them to allow for expansion and contraction. To disguise the gap, run a felt-tip marker along the seam.

3 TACK THE SHEET IN PLACE.

Align the panel so it is plumb and drive three or more finishing or color-matched paneling nails halfway in along the top edge of the panel. With the panel dangling, compress the adhesive behind it by hammering on the surface with a block of wood wrapped in cloth.

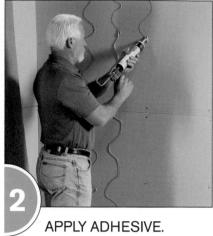

2 APPLY ADHESIVE.

Using a caulking gun, apply a ½-inch bead of panel adhesive on the wall in a wavy pattern so there is no gap larger than 8 inches between adhesive beads. (A large caulking gun that holds quart tubes may be a worthwhile investment.) Press the panel back in place and elevate it above the floor about ½ inch.

4 ALLOW ADHESIVE TO SET AND ATTACH PANEL.

Pull out the bottom of the panel and insert a spacer to keep it away from the wall while the adhesive sets up. After the time specified for the adhesive (typically 3 minutes), press the panel against the wall and drive nails every 8 inches along the edges and every 12 inches into intermediate studs.

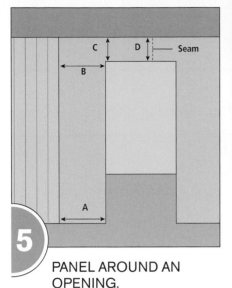

5 PANEL AROUND AN OPENING.

To panel around a door or window, measure over from the last panel installed. Measure up from the floor or down from the ceiling to find the height of the opening. Measure in the A, B, C, D sequence shown. If possible, lay out panels so their seams fall over the center of openings. Remember to allow a $\frac{1}{16}$-inch gap between panels.

6 FIT THE LAST PANEL.

For the last piece, you'll need to precision-cut a panel to fit neatly against the inside edge of the wall. Most likely, the corner will not be plumb, so measure from the previous panel to the corner at several points along the panel edge and draw a line on the last panel with a straightedge. Cut with a circular saw or, for curves, a jigsaw. When cutting with either of these tools, cut with the back of the panel facing up to prevent splintering the good face.

7 FINE-TUNE THE EDGE.

It may take several attempts before you get a panel to fit against an irregular corner. Be conservative in your cutting; you can always cut more, but you can't make the sheet bigger. Use a block plane or surface-forming tool to shave off small amounts of material. Hold the tool at an angle so the bulk of the material is cut from the back of the panel, leaving a thin edge at the front surface that can easily be trimmed for final fitting.

8 MAKE CUTOUTS.

To cut openings for electrical outlets, measure the distance between the last panel installed and the right and left edges of the outlet. Measure from the floor to the top and bottom of the outlet box too. Transfer the measurements to the panel, and cut the opening with a jigsaw.

9 SCRIBE AROUND COMPLEX OBSTRUCTIONS.

To cut around a fireplace surround or other ornamentation, measure the distance from the last installed sheet to the farthest point along the structure. Measure the height of the structure, allowing for the gap along the floor. Transfer your measurements to the paneling, connect the cut lines with a straightedge, and saw out the bulk of the waste area.

Temporarily nail up the sheet so it is plumb and alongside the structure at the proper elevation. Set a compass (see pages 112–113) to the width the sheet needs to move to meet the last panel installed and scribe the contours onto the sheet.

Make the cut using a saber saw with a fine-tooth blade or a coping saw. Fit the panel and make fine adjustments with a utility knife. Secure the panel in place.

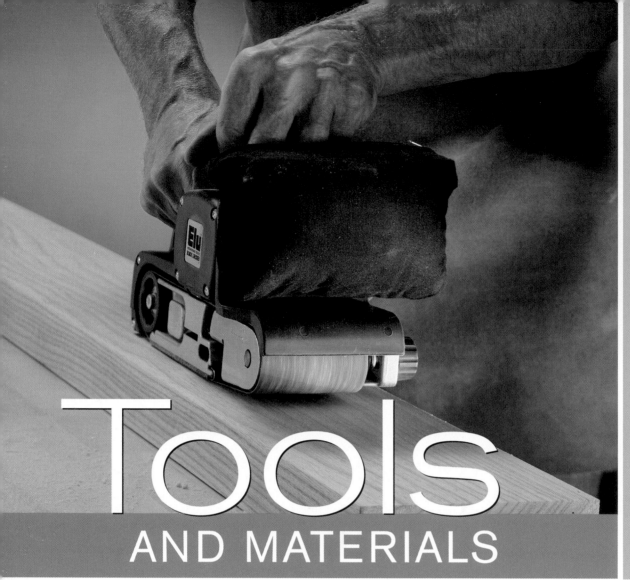

<

WORK FASTER WITH POWER
When a project calls for a lengthy or repeated action, a power tool speeds up the work and can save you some tedious work.

Tools
AND MATERIALS

One thing to remember when starting any project is that no matter how complex it may seem, it can be broken down into smaller, simpler projects, then reduced further to the tools and materials of construction. Understanding the tools and materials determines the success or failure of every project.

This chapter identifies the different tools required for most carpentry projects. Learn about hand tools, basic power tools, and specialized power tools. Some tools you may already have. Others you may want to purchase. Specialty tools tend to be job specific and expensive, so rather than purchasing them, you may want to rent them from a local rental store.

A discussion on organizing your tools presents ideas on how to avoid clutter so that you can find the right tool when you need it, saving time and frustration.

Knowing how to select materials impacts both the stability and durability of any completed project. You will learn how to select and buy lumber, the difference between softwoods and hardwoods, how to properly store and handle materials, and the right types of fasteners to use, and you'll see a sampling of available hardware. Armed with this knowledge, you can confidently begin any carpentry project.

<

USE THE RIGHT TOOLS

The right tools and workspace make any job easier. Beginning on page 82 are suggestions for assembling the tools necessary to complete the projects in this book, as well as most home repair or remodeling jobs. Turn to page 88 for recommendations on how to organize an efficient, comfortable work space.

>

FIT TOOLS TO YOUR NEEDS

Consider your workspace and project needs when purchasing power tools. Freestanding tools are more powerful and accurate than handheld or benchtop versions. Benchtop and handheld models are convenient for small spaces and limited budgets. See pages 85–87 for more information about selecting power tools.

SELECTING HAND TOOLS

The right hand tool makes your job easier and yields better results. Hand tools are relatively inexpensive, so it's easy to gather a collection. To avoid filling the basement with tools that will never be used, assemble a basic tool kit and add to your collection when the job at hand requires a new tool.

Typically the top-of-the-line contractor-type tool will be of higher quality than an average homeowner needs, but inexpensive tools will not perform well. Your best choice is a midpriced model. If you need a tool to complete an unusual task and probably won't need it very often, consider renting it. If you do buy it, go with a less expensive version.

Few tools see more action than the flexible **tape measure.** Buy a 25-foot one with a 1-inch-wide blade; this will extend farther and last longer than a ¾-inch one. Some carpenters prefer a folding ruler for smaller jobs. Purchase one with a metal pullout extension for making precise inside-to-inside measurements (see page 106).

A **framing square** (also called a carpenter's square) is used to check corners for square and to mark for rafters and stringers. More often, you'll need a smaller square. A triangular **speed square** is easy to use, allows you to quickly figure 45-degree-angle cuts, and holds its shape after getting banged around. It slips into your back pocket and is handy for quickly marking cut lines on planks and framing material. A **combination square** is helpful for scribing lines (see page 107). A **T-bevel** can be set to duplicate an angle.

Plumb and level large and small projects with a **carpenter's level.** A 2- or 4-foot model works well for most projects. A **plumb bob** establishes true vertical lines. Snap long, straight lines with a **chalk line.** A chalk line also can double as a plumb bob.

Even if you do most of your cutting with power tools, a **handsaw** still comes in handy, especially a smaller saw that fits into a toolbox. For accurate miter cuts, use a **backsaw** and **miter box.** Use a **drywall saw** to cut curves in drywall. To make rough curved cuts in wood, choose a **keyhole saw.** Cut intricate and precise curves in thin materials with a **coping saw.**

Wood chisels enable you to shape mortises and make rough notches in places where a saw will not reach. Choose chisels with metal-capped handles. Have a **utility knife** close at hand for razor-sharp cuts. Most people prefer one with a retractable blade. To shave wood along the length of a board, use a **plane** for the smoothest cut. For rough shaping, use a **rasp** or a **wood file.**

Buy a **hammer** that is comfortable and solidly built. The most popular model weighs 16 ounces and has curved claws. You'll find a variety of specialty hammers, including framing and wallboard hammers. Stick to the basic curved-claw hammer. To sink the heads of finishing nails below the surface of the work, use a **nail set.**

Have plenty of **screwdrivers** on hand; get various sizes of both phillips-tip and straight-tipped types or buy a combination screwdriver that has four tips in one tool. Make pilot holes for small screws with an **awl.**

To fasten nuts, bolts, and lag screws, use an **adjustable wrench.** For holding pieces of wood firmly, have **C-clamps** of various sizes handy. A pair of **locking pliers** helps to hold fasteners or pieces of wood tight while you work.

Tongue-and-groove pliers are one of the most useful tools you can buy, so it makes sense to pay extra for a high-quality pair. They grab almost anything firmly and work well for pulling nails. **Lineman's pliers** enable you to grab items tightly from the

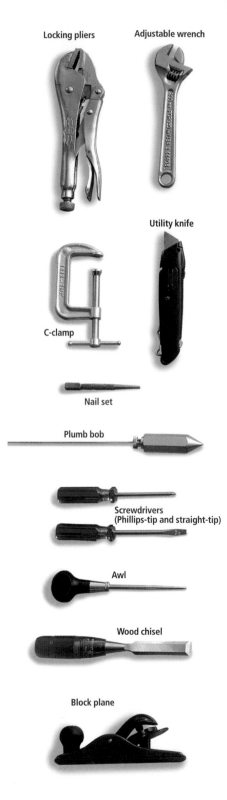

Locking pliers

Adjustable wrench

Utility knife

C-clamp

Nail set

Plumb bob

Screwdrivers
(Phillips-tip and straight-tip)

Awl

Wood chisel

Block plane

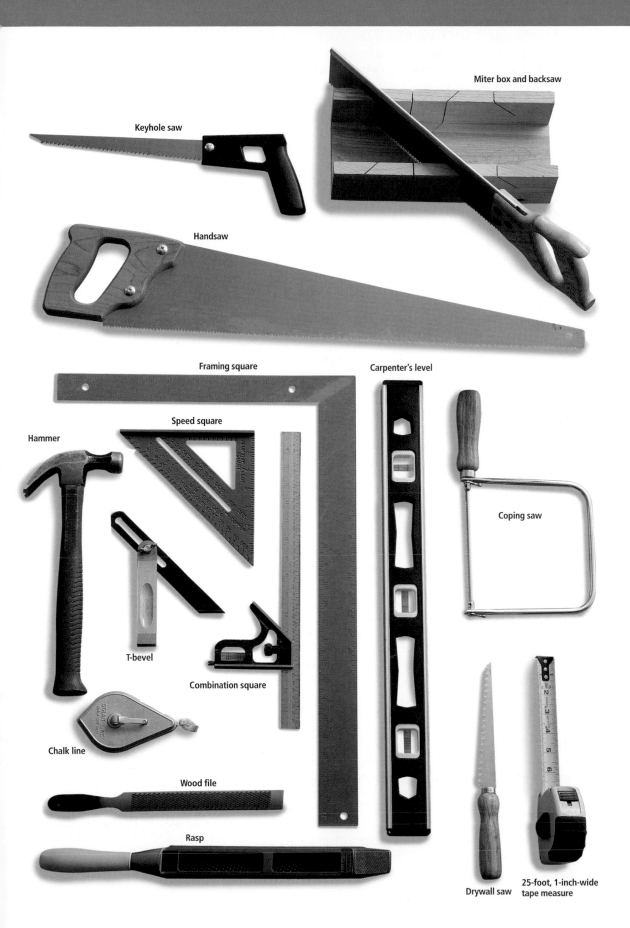

Keyhole saw

Miter box and backsaw

Handsaw

Framing square

Carpenter's level

Speed square

Hammer

Coping saw

T-bevel

Combination square

Chalk line

Wood file

Drywall saw

25-foot, 1-inch-wide
tape measure

Rasp

Selecting hand tools *(continued)*

front rather than the side of the tool and also will cut nails or screws. **Side-cutting pliers** enable you to cut nails nearly flush to the surface. They also are useful for grabbing the pointed ends of finishing nails to pull them out of the back of molding without marring the face. **Locking pliers** are handy for gripping tightly and pulling.

A **flat pry bar** is indispensable. With it you can pry off fastened lumber pieces with minimal damage to the wood. It also is handy for levering heavy objects into place (for example, reattaching a door on its hinges).

A **cat's paw** (also called a nail puller) makes it easy to pull nails, although it will damage the wood (see page 136). It's indispensable if you are planning any demolition.

For patching damaged walls and for taping drywall, have a variety of sizes of **taping knives** to apply wallboard compound (see pages 76–77). If you have 6-, 8-, and 12-inch blades you will be prepared to tape or patch almost any surface. If you have a lot of drywall to cut, you'll thank yourself for buying a **drywall square.** You'll also find it is very useful for marking cut lines on pieces of plywood.

Sanding large wall and ceiling areas is much easier if you have a **pole sander.** Buy a smaller sanding block for detail work (see page 151).

Use a **caulking gun** to fill cracks with caulk or to apply construction adhesive. Purchase a **staple gun** to attach sheets of plastic or felt or to install fiberglass insulation.

A **surface-forming tool** can substitute for a plane when working with wood, but it will not cut as straight or as smooth. It is more versatile, however, and comes in handy for fine-tuning anything from foamboard to wallboard.

When you need to stabilize something that is too thick to handle with a C-clamp, use a quick-fitting **adjustable clamp.** To clamp a straightedge in place or to hold thin materials that might be marred by a C-clamp (see pages 82–83) or adjustable clamp, use a **spring clamp** (see page 138 for other specialized clamps).

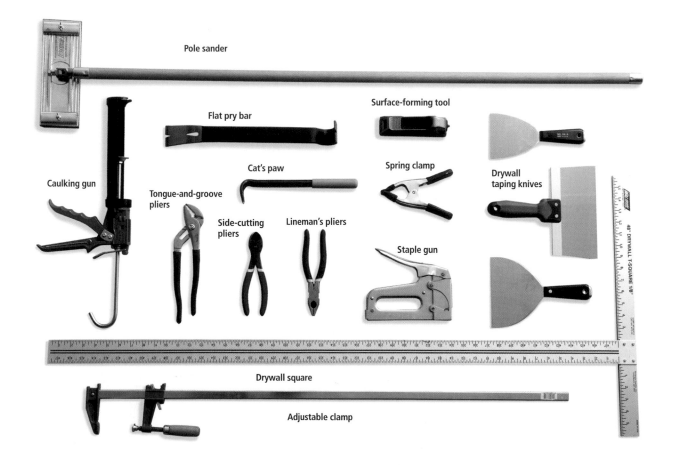

Pole sander

Flat pry bar

Surface-forming tool

Caulking gun

Tongue-and-groove pliers

Cat's paw

Side-cutting pliers

Lineman's pliers

Spring clamp

Drywall taping knives

Staple gun

Drywall square

Adjustable clamp

BASIC POWER TOOLS

A circular saw, a power drill, and a jigsaw (sometimes called a saber saw) are musts for your basic tool kit. With the two saws you can make straight and curved cuts quickly in almost any material. The drill lets you make holes of almost any size and drive screws quickly and easily. With these three tools you can handle almost any household carpentry job.

A **circular saw** crosscuts, angle-cuts, rips (cuts lengthwise), and even bevels lumber easily and cleanly. Don't worry if the saw has a plastic housing; many plastics are very strong. Do take a look at the metal baseplate. A baseplate made of thin, stamped metal can warp; look for a thicker base made of extruded or cast metal. A saw that takes 7¼-inch blades is the usual choice. It allows you to cut to a depth of about 2½ inches at 90 degrees and to cut through a piece of 2× lumber even when the blade is set at 45 degrees.

Horsepower is not important when choosing a circular saw. Instead look at the amperage and the type of bearings. A low-cost saw pulls only 9 or 10 amps and usually has sleeve bearings. This means less power, a shorter life because it heats up easily, and less precise cuts because the blade may wobble somewhat. Better saws are rated at 12 or 13 amps and often have ball bearings. This combination of extra power and smoother operation makes for long life and more precise cutting. Worm-drive saws, which are the most powerful saws, are heavy and relatively expensive. As is often the case, a midpriced saw is your best choice.

Be sure to get a variable-speed, reversible **power drill.** Unless you will be doing heavy-duty work, you don't need one with a ½-inch chuck; a ⅜-inch one is fine. Buy a drill that pulls at least 3.5 amps. A keyless chuck simplifies changing bits, but some people prefer a keyed chuck for a tighter grip on the bit.

A **cordless drill** frees you to work without the mess of electrical cords. Buy one rated at least 9.6 volts, preferably more. If possible, get an extra battery pack so you won't have to wait for a battery to charge.

When buying a **jigsaw,** examine the baseplate and the mechanism for adjusting it. On less expensive saws, these are flimsy and eventually wobble, making it difficult to keep the blade aligned vertically. Variable speed is a useful option. A saw that draws 3 amps or more handles most cutting jobs.

Circular saw

Cordless drill

Power drill

Jigsaw

SELECTING SPECIALIZED POWER TOOLS

The more carpentry jobs you take on, the more power tools you will need or want to own. Many of these are high-priced items, so research carefully before making a purchase. If the tool is one you will turn to often, pay extra money to get a high-quality one that will last. If you will use it only rarely, settle for a lesser quality tool.

To determine the quality of a tool, check the amperage rather than the horsepower. Compare models and avoid buying the one with the lowest amperage rating. A plastic housing is not necessarily a sign of poor quality. But do check any mechanisms and metal attachments to see if they're solid. A tool with ball bearings runs smoother and lasts longer than one with other types of bearings.

For quick sanding of large areas, nothing beats a **belt sander.** Make sure it uses belts that are easily available—3×24 inches is the most common size. A good belt sander is fairly heavy and has a large dust collector. You can switch from rough to fine sanding belts; however, because a belt sander is difficult to handle for fine work, you probably will want to use another method for the final sanding—either a hand-sanding block or a smaller mechanized sander, such as a **random-orbit sander.** It works by moving rapidly in overlapping orbits. Some people prefer the finish of an older-style orbital sander, which moves back and forth. Some units switch from orbital to a nearly straight action.

With a **router** you can form a wide variety of decorative or joinery profiles on lumber. Routers are either fixed-base models, which are ideal for edge work, or plunge routers. The head of a plunge router moves up and down on the base, so you can start routing anywhere on a board.

If you plan a project that calls for joining two pieces of lumber side by side, a **biscuit joiner** produces professional-looking results with ease (see page 146).

Need to drill holes that are precisely vertical? You can purchase a **drill press** or a drill stand that uses a regular power drill. A stand is less expensive than a drill press but takes more time to set up and use.

For demolition and extensive remodeling work, you'll want a **reciprocating saw.** It can make cuts in places where no other saw will reach. If you need to remove portions of walls or floors, this tool can save you a lot of time and frustration.

Random-orbit sander

Router

Belt sander

Biscuit joiner

Reciprocating saw

Drill press

If you have to cut a lot of molding or exterior siding, consider a **power mitersaw.** This tool (also called a chopsaw or cutoff saw) resembles a circular saw mounted on a pivot assembly. It makes quick, precise crosscuts and miter cuts. Make sure you get a saw large enough to cut all the way through the stock you want to cut; a 10-inch blade handles most projects. A compound mitersaw or sliding compound mitersaw offers the greatest versatility.

Use a **bench grinder** to sharpen tools and shape metal objects. Bolt it to your work bench, and it will be ready to use at a moment's notice.

With a good **tablesaw** you can make straight, long cuts. Use it for dado cuts as well. It also works for crosscuts and miter cuts (see page 123), but not as easily as a power mitersaw. Choose a model that has a solid table that will not wiggle as you work on it, a fence that stays firmly in place, and a powerful motor. Keep in mind that you will need a good deal of room in your shop if you are going to use a tablesaw to cut sheets of plywood or long pieces of lumber.

A **radial-arm saw** is a general-purpose power saw. It is best suited to crosscuts, but it can make ripcuts too. A sliding compound mitersaw often saws miters and crosscuts more accurately and a tablesaw is more convenient for ripcuts.

Power mitersaw

Bench grinder

Radial-arm saw

Tablesaw

(see page 123)

TOOL SAFETY TIPS

Safety is the result of following guidelines and exercising common sense. When working with a power tool, just one moment's lapse of concentration can lead to serious injury. To minimize risks with power tools, keep the following guidelines in mind:

- Use tools only for the jobs they were designed to do. If a tool came with an instruction manual, take the time to read it to find out what the tool will do and what it will not do.

- Check on the condition of a tool before using it. A dull cutting edge or a loose-fitting hammerhead, for example, spells trouble. Also inspect the cord of a power tool to make sure it's not damaged.

- Don't work with tools if you're tired or in a hurry.

- Don't work with tools if you have recently been drinking alcohol.

- Wear goggles whenever the operation you are performing could result in eye injury.

- The safety mechanisms on power tools are there for your protection. Don't tamper with or remove them from the tool.

- Don't wear loose-fitting clothes or dangling jewelry while you are using tools.

- Keep people, especially children, at a safe distance while you're using any tool. Before you let children use a tool, instruct them on how to operate it and supervise them as they work.

- Before servicing or adjusting a power tool, unplug it and allow moving parts to stop.

ORGANIZING YOUR TOOLS

If you're serious about doing carpentry work around your house, you will need a convenient, comfortable, well-organized place in which to work and store the tools and materials you will accumulate. Your carpentry headquarters can be a full-fledged shop, or it may be a simple tool container and a corner set aside for lumber. But you need a work center—and the sooner, the better.

You can build your workshop in a basement, garage, seldom-used room, or even a closet or attic. A basement has several advantages. It's off the beaten path, so you needn't worry about disrupting family activities as you work. In most homes it's also one of the few areas with a sizable amount of unused space—an important factor if you want to use stationary power tools. However, if your basement tends to get wet or if it will be difficult to get sheet goods into it, you may want to investigate other areas.

Once you've decided on the tools you would like to have, plan your space carefully. Here are some tips:

- Make sure there is plenty of light. Large fluorescent fixtures usually work best. Make sure the lights are positioned so you won't accidentally bump the bulbs.
- Run at least one 20-amp electrical circuit with a ground-fault circuit interrupter to the shop to provide power for your heavy-duty tools. Large shops should have separate circuits for tools and lights. Position electrical outlets strategically around the workshop so power is never far away.
- Give yourself a way to easily carry your tools from place to place. An apron made to fit a five-gallon bucket has room for a drill, power cord, and other large tools in the middle and smaller tools in pockets around the outside. You may prefer a toolbox for smaller items.
- Have at least two sawhorses on hand. Use these to support bulky sheet goods and lengths of lumber while you're working on them in the shop and to help you work at job sites.
- Make it as easy as possible to keep your shop clean or have a broom, dustpan, and portable vacuum on hand. If you do a lot of woodworking, buy a dust collector—a central vacuum with tubes running to stationary tools. Have large garbage containers you can easily carry out to the trash.
- If you have a forced-air furnace, make sure the dust you make cannot get sucked into it and change the filters often.

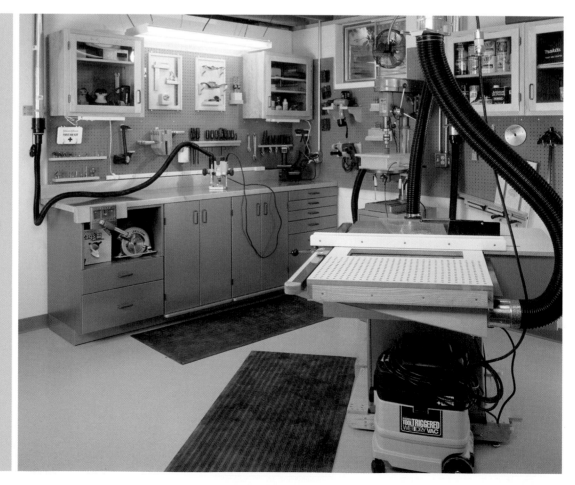

> **WELL-PLANNED WORKSHOP**
> This well-designed workshop makes it a pleasure to complete virtually any project. The ideal workshop should contain ample bright light, grounded electrical outlets throughout the room and along the edges of workbenches to avoid a jumble of extension cords, wall-mounted and enclosed storage for equipment and materials, workbenches, and easy-to-clean, soft floor mats of a durable material such as rubber or vinyl.

- Make sure the work area has adequate ventilation. If possible, install an exhaust fan that can change the air in the shop every four minutes. The cubic feet (length times width times height) in your shop will determine the size of the fan needed.
- The workbench is the activity hub of every shop. A full-size workbench typically measures 6 to 8 feet long, 24 to 36 inches deep, and 40 to 42 inches high. You may want to make it the exact height of your tablesaw or radial-arm saw. This makes it easy to handle sheets of plywood for cutting, using the bench as an additional cutting support. If you have limited space, it may make sense to have a smaller bench on wheels so you can store it out of the way. You may want to include a storage shelf below the workbench surface area.

See pages 18–19 for how to build a workbench.
- Attach a sheet of perforated hardboard to the wall near your workbench for hanging tools. Install the board so it extends 1 or 2 inches out from the wall so tool hooks can be inserted. If the hooks tend to pop out every time you remove a tool, glue them in place with construction adhesive or hot glue.
- Provide plenty of storage for your tools and materials. See page 99 for how to store lumber.

WORKSHOP ORGANIZERS

You need a good storage system if you want to store all your nails, screws, small tools, and various pieces of hardware so they will be easy to find. In addition to ready-made organizers, consider these possibilities:

- Nail glass jar lids to an overhead surface so you can reach up and unscrew jars full of fasteners or hardware. The great advantage here is that you can see what's inside each container.

- Keep items visible. Either use open shelves or place the shelves at eye level so it's easy to find items you've stored.

KEEP YOUR TOOLS ORGANIZED.

Many options are available for organizing tools and materials. Tool pouches or belts let you carry tools with you as you work on a project, eliminating the need to interrupt your work to get items you forgot. Keep tools in the same pockets all the time so you'll always reach for the right tool. Tool bags allow you to tote all of the tools you need to your work area but free you from the constant weight of a tool pouch or belt. Side pockets store smaller, frequently used items such as hammers and screwdrivers. The main compartment is large enough to comfortably house a power tool in addition to larger hand tools. Plastic organizer cases are great for storing hardware and fasteners in separate compartments. These cases are ideal for holding small numbers of numerous materials, rather than nails by the pound necessary for a big job.

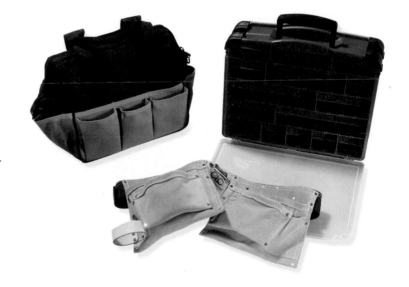

As you learn carpentry techniques, it's important to become familiar with the characteristics and uses of various types of lumber and how to choose the wood that will work best for a particular project.

There are two basic types of lumber: softwoods, from coniferous trees, and hardwoods, from deciduous trees. Wood is graded according to how many knots it has and the quality of its surface (see the chart *below* for the most common grades). Some lumberyards have their own grading systems, but they usually simply rename these standard grades.

No matter what species of lumber you buy, be on the lookout for the types of wood problems shown at *right*. A board that is heavily twisted, bowed, cupped, or crooked usually is not usable, although some bows will lie down as you nail them in place. Knots are only a cosmetic problem unless they are loose and likely to pop out. Checking, which is a rift in the surface, also is only cosmetic. Splits cannot be repaired and will widen in time. Cut them off.

The nominal dimensions of wood are used when ordering lumber. Keep in mind that the actual dimensions of the lumber will be smaller (see the chart on page 91). Large quantities of lumber are sometimes figured by the board foot. A board foot is the wood equivalent of a piece 12 nominal inches square and 1 inch thick (see chart at bottom). Most lumberyards will not require you to figure board feet.

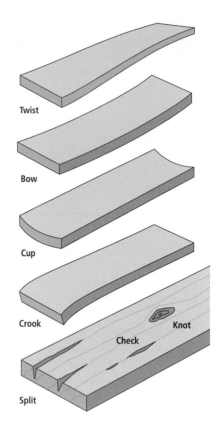

Twist

Bow

Cup

Crook

Knot

Check

Split

SOME COMMON GRADES OF WOOD

Grade	Characteristics
Clear	Has no knots.
Select or select structural	Very high-quality wood. Broken down into Nos. 1–3 or grades A–D; the lower grades will have more knots.
No. 2 common	Has tight knots, no major blemishes; good for shelving.
No. 3 common	Some knots may be loose; often blemished or damaged.
Construction or standard	Good strength; used for general framing.
Utility	Economy grade used for rough framing.

To determine board feet, multiply nominal width by nominal thickness in inches. Then multiply by the actual length in feet and divide by 12.

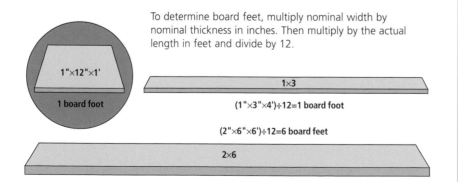

1"×12"×1'

1 board foot

1×3

(1"×3"×4')÷12=1 board foot

(2"×6"×6')÷12=6 board feet

2×6

INSPECT BEFORE BUYING

If you order lumber by telephone, you will get someone else's choice of boards, not your own. Lumberyards usually have plenty of substandard wood lying around. The only way to be sure you do not get some of it is to pick out the boards yourself. Some lumberyards will not allow you to sort through the stacks because they want to keep wood neatly stacked—the only way to keep lumber from warping. But they should at least let you stand by and approve the selection. Failing that, confirm that you can return boards you don't like.

LUMBER SELECTOR

Type	Description and Uses	Nominal Sizes	Actual Sizes
Furring	 Rough wood of small dimensions. For furring drywall and paneling, interior and exterior trim, shimming, stakes, crates, light-duty frames, latticework, and edging.	1×2 1×3	¾×1½ ¾×2½
Finish lumber	 Smooth-finished lumber. For paneling, trim, shelving, light framing, structural finishing, forming, siding, decking, casing, valances, cabinets, built-ins, and furniture.	1×4 1×6 1×8 1×10 1×12	¾×3½ ¾×5½ ¾×7¼ ¾×9¼ ¾×11¼
Tongue-and-groove	 Tongues and grooves connect into each other for a tight fit. For decorative interior wall treatments, exterior siding, flooring, and subflooring.	1×4 1×6 1×8	Actual sizes vary from mill to mill.
Shiplap	 One edge fits on top of the other. For decorative wall treatments, siding, decking, exterior sheathing, and subflooring.	1×4 1×6 1×8	¾×3⅛ ¾×5⅛ ¾×6⅞
Dimensional lumber	 Studs are usually 2×4, sometimes 2×6. Planks are 6 or more inches wide. For structural framing (wall studs, ceiling and floor joists, rafters, headers, top and bottom plates), structural finishing, forming, exterior decking and fencing, and stair components (stringers, steps).	2×2 2×3 2×4 2×6 2×8 2×10 2×12 4×4 4×6 6×6	1½×1½ 1½×2½ 1½×3½ 1½×5½ 1½×7¼ 1½×9¼ 1½×11¼ 3½×3½ 3½×5½ 5½×5½
Glue-laminate	 Layers of dimensional lumber laid flat on top of each other and laminated into one solid piece. Used for rafters, joists, and beams. Can be stained for exposed beams.	4×10 4×12 6×10 6×12	3½×9 3½×12 5½×9 5½×12
Microlaminate	 Veneers glued together with crossing grains like plywood, only thicker. For rafters, joists, and beams.	4×12	3½×11⅜

SELECTING WOOD

Just as you spend time considering your choices for a new wall paint color and flooring options to update a room, you should take the time to investigate your options before selecting a wood species and grade for your carpentry or woodworking project. Each type of wood has its own characteristics. The characteristics of wood will impact how you work with the wood as you build your project, and its characteristics will greatly impact the finished appearance of the project. Before you make a trip to the local lumberyard, home improvement center, or hardware store, it is important for you to understand the basic characteristics and common uses of the wood species you are considering. The next several pages detail information about the most common types of softwoods and hardwoods.

In part, the selection of wood for a project should be based on whether the wood is suitable for the particular use you are considering. For example, pine is relatively soft and weak, so it is not a good choice for a bookcase to house a comprehensive collection of literary classics. Oak, which is much stronger, may be the perfect choice.

Your choice of wood, however, should also involve aesthetics. Oak may prove to be an excellent choice for strong, sturdy bookcases, but you may not care for the open grain of oak. You may opt for maple, cherry or walnut instead. Following are some specific items to consider as you choose the ideal wood for your project.

Consider the wood's resistance to dents and scratches. Selecting a softwood or hardwood that has a relatively soft or medium hardness probably does not make sense for a high-traffic area or a location that will take a lot of abuse, such as a countertop or cutting block Maple,

for example is among the hardest of domestic woods—you may even have heard it referred to as "hard maple" or "rock maple." That's why most chopping blocks are maple.

Some wood species are said to have better "workability" than others. This means you'll find them easier to saw, chisel plane or drive screws into. In general, softer woods are easier to work with than harder woods, but be aware that workability can vary greatly from board to board. Straight-grained boards are much easier to work than boards that have lots of knots or wild swirling grain. Of course, wild grain can also add lots of visual interest.

Consider the grade of wood, no matter the species. (See page 90 for information about the most common grades of wood.) Using wood free from defects may not be important for all projects. For example, unfinished basement storage shelves require sound wood, but not knot-free wood. Some defects can even add aesthetic value to a finished project. A knot might give the touch of rustic character you want for a door in a country-theme interior. Other projects—such as a showpiece cabinet finished with a natural stain and installed in a main living area—requires a top grade of wood. Look at the selection of wood available at a

PRO TIPS AND TERMS

Use this information from carpentry and woodworking pros to help you select and purchase wood for your next project.

- The price for a given species of wood may vary greatly by region. Local woods usually are less expensive than species that need to be shipped across the country, or the world. You'll pay significantly less for redwood in California than you will in Pennsylvania. But Pennsylvanians are more likely to find a good price for indigenous black cherry.

- You can select for grain and then stain. If for example, your heart, but not your pocketbook is set on cherry, take a look at birch. The grain and hardness are very similar. With the right stain, you can achieve the cherry look you're after.

- Quartersawn lumber is less likely to warp than plain-sawn wood. To tell the difference, look at the end of the board: In quartersawn boards the growth rings will be fairly straight and roughly perpendicular to the face. In a plainsawn board the rings will curve toward one face of the board. Unfortunately, quartersawing yields much less useable lumber from a log and so quartersawn boards are and more rare and costly.

- For some lost reason, hardwood lumber thickness is always given in quarters of an inch. So, you don't buy a 2-thick oak board. You buy 8/4 oak.

- Hardwood lumber is sold by the "board foot." This is any volume equal to 1 foot by 1 foot by 1 inch. So a 6-inch-wide piece of 4/4 cherry that's 4 feet long is equal to 2 board feet, while a 6-inch-wide piece of 8/4 cherry that's 4 feet long is equal to 4 board feet. BF= L(ft.)XW(in.)XT(in.)/12.

local lumberyard or hardware store. The colors, grains, and textures of the various woods can impact the overall look of your project. For most projects, you'll want to avoid wood with numerous knots, pitch streaks, splits, checks, and stains. Even for a rustic project, you'll want to avoid wood that is heavily twisted, bowed, cupped or crooked.

The stability of wood determines its tendency to shrink and warp. Wood for interior construction typically has a moisture content between 6 and 8 percent, but the moisture content may be significantly higher, causing significant shrinking and warping problems that over time can undermine the success of your project. Check with the supplier of the wood. Remember that even properly dried wood shrinks and swells in response to seasonal changes of humidity and temperature. Finishes don't completely stop water absorption and emission, but they do reduce the amount of moisture that moves through the wood, thus making the wood more stable. Heavy hardwoods respond more to changes in humidity and temperature than lighter woods.

Most hardwoods are too dense to drive screws or nails into without predrilling. You may want to do a test using a piece of scrap lumber to determine whether you will need to predrill holes to avoid splitting and cracking the wood, and to avoid bending or breaking the fasteners. See page 133 for more information about pilot holes.

No matter what type and grade of wood you select for your project, always sand wood before finishing to provide a smooth surface. Sand with the grain, never across. Start with a coarse grit sandpaper and slowly work towards a fine grit that will provide a smooth surface. For more tips on sanding, see page 151. Even wood that will be painted needs to be sanded with medium-grit sandpaper to remove "mill marks"—ripples caused by the machine that planed the wood to size.

To protect your wood project and to enhance its beauty, complete your work by applying the right finish. Clear finishes enhance the natural beauty of wood. A wide variety of stains are available to color the wood. If painting, select a high quality paint

SOFTWOOD SELECTOR

Species	Characteristics	Common Uses
Cedar, cypress	Similar to redwood—only the darker wood is resistant to rot. Weak, brittle; resists warping; pleasant aroma; easy to work.	Siding, paneling, rough trim, roof shingles and shakes, decks.
Fir, larch	Heavy, very strong, hard; holds nails well; good resistance to warping and shrinkage; somewhat difficult to work.	Framing studs, joists, posts, and beams; flooring; subflooring.
"Hem/fir"	A general classification that takes in a variety of species, including hemlock and fir. Lightweight, soft, fairly strong; warps easily; may shrink; easy to work.	Framing, exterior fascia, flooring, subflooring, trim.
Pine	From Eastern, Northern, and Western trees. Lightweight, soft, fairly weak; good resistance to warping but with a tendency to shrink; easy to work.	Paneling, trim (molding), flooring, cabinets.
Redwood	Durable and resistant to rot and insects if you get the darker-colored heartwood. Light, soft, not as strong as fir or Southern pine; tendency to split; easy to work.	Exterior posts and beams, siding, paneling, decks, fences.
Southern pine	Very hard, stiff, excellent strength; holds nails well; has a tendency to crack, splinter, warp; works with average ease.	Framing, subflooring.
Spruce	Lightweight, soft, fairly strong; resistant to splitting and warping; easy to work.	Framing, flooring, subflooring, trim (molding).
Treated lumber	Several species can be treated—most often fir, "hem/fir," and Southern pine are used. Green or brown color will fade in time, leaving the wood a dirty gray; extremely resistant to rot and insects. Workability depends on species.	Bottom framing plates that rest on concrete; other framing that might come into contact with water; decks; fences.

that resists abrasion and denting while being washable for easy cleaning. See page 153 for detailed information about filling and finishing your projects.

Softwoods

Unless you're installing major structural components, such as floor or ceiling joists, that will bear significant weight, you can't make a serious mistake when buying softwoods. In most cases, you simply want to buy the wood that looks best or is the least expensive.

Softwood usually is less expensive than hardwood because it comes from trees that grow faster. In general, the disadvantage of softwood is evident in its name: It actually is soft. If you use softwood for furniture and other objects that will get handled and

bumped, plan on applying a hard finish or paint. Even then, the wood will not be as durable as hardwood.

Most retail suppliers stock only a few species of softwood. The chart below summarizes the chief characteristics of each. In most cases, you'll be choosing between grades of lumber rather than species. Which grade you choose depends on the nature of your project.

Softwood grading is difficult because several grading systems exist. Most often, however, you'll find two general classifications: select and common.

Use select lumber, which comes in several subgrades, for trim or cabinetry where finished appearance counts. For all other projects, common lumber will do nicely. Common lumber is graded as No. 1, No. 2, and No. 3.

With some suppliers, you can dispense with the grades and talk about more straightforward categories, such as "clear" (without knots) and "tight-knot" (having only small knots without cracks).

Of course, the better the grade— that is, the fewer the defects— the more you pay for the product. Often, however, a better grade is only slightly more expensive. Once you

gain some experience, if you sort through the lumber rack carefully, you often can find pieces that are out of their class—for instance, a piece of No. 2 common that actually could have been classified as select.

Hardwoods

You can buy various types of plastic-laminated products made to look like hardwood, but there is no substitute for the real thing. Hardwood flooring and trim give a home elegance unmatched by any other product. For furniture and cabinetry, nothing quite measures up in appearance and durability.

Unfortunately, hardwood trees grow slowly, so prices tend to be higher than they are for softwood. But prices fluctuate widely from year to year, and often the difference is surprisingly small. Oak flooring, for example, sometimes costs less than softwood flooring.

The more expensive hardwoods are milled to make use of virtually every splinter of wood. Instead of the standard sizes, some hardwoods are sold in pieces of varying lengths and widths. Sometimes the boards are smooth-surfaced on only two sides (S2S), leaving the edges rough.

CREATIVE WOOD SOURCES
If your basic carpentry pursuits leads you to more serious woodworking projects, one potential source for wood is trees downed by a storm. Make sure you receive permission from the homeowners or local officials. The wood from a tree such as this would have to be milled and dried before use.

HARDNESS OF SELECTED WOODS

Softwoods		
Soft	**Medium**	**Hard**
Western red cedar	Pine White fir	Douglas fir

Hardwoods		
Soft	**Medium**	**Hard**
Poplar Basswood Willow	Black ash Cherry Paper birch Silver maple	Black walnut Red and white oak Yellow birch White ash

HARDWOOD SELECTOR

Species	Characteristics	Common Uses
Birch	Hard, strong; fine-grained; resists shrinking and warping; holds paint well. Similar in color to maple—sometimes used as a more economical replacement. Finishes fairly well; hard to cut.	Paintable cabinets, paneling, trim, furniture.
Mahogany	Durable; fine-grained; resistant to shrinking, warping, and swelling. Finishes well; easy to cut. (Not to be confused with lauan mahogany, a less expensive material that is used for veneers and plywoods.)	Fine furniture, cabinets, millwork, veneers.
Maple	Extremely hard, strong; pieces with bird's-eye or wavy grains are highly prized. Color ranges from reddish to nearly white in color. Finishes well; hard to cut.	Flooring (basketball and bowling alley floors are made of maple), butcher blocks, veneers, countertops, millwork, and molding.
Poplar	Lightweight, soft for a hardwood; fine-grained. White to yellow-brown in color. Paints well; easy to cut.	Paintable furniture, cabinets, trim, paneling, places where a less expensive hardwood will do.
Red oak	Hard, strong, rigid; pronounced open grain; resists warping but may shrink if not well-dried. Reddish color. Finishes well; moderately hard to cut.	Flooring, doors, furniture, cabinets, molding, stair rails.
Walnut	Hard, heavy, extra strong; fairly pronounced, straight grain; resists warping and shrinking. Light to dark brown in color. Finishes well; cuts fairly easily.	Fine furniture, cabinets, millwork, paneling, inlays, veneers.
White oak	Hard, strong; open grain but not as pronounced as red oak; resists shrinking and warping. Golden color. Finishes well; moderately hard to cut.	Better than red oak for flooring—less variation in color. Millwork, molding, furniture, cabinets, doors, stair rails, balusters.

Hardwoods may be priced by the board foot (see page 90).

Hardwood grading differs from that of softwoods. It is based primarily on the amount of clear surface area on the board. The best grade is FAS (firsts and seconds), which is the most knot-free. Select boards have defects on one side only; No. 1 common has tiny, tight knots; No. 2 common has larger knots.

Most lumberyards and home centers can't afford to maintain an extensive inventory of hardwood lumber and generally stock only a limited assortment of a few species. For the best selection, find stores that specialize in hardwoods. They stock or can order a wide selection of species.

HARDWOOD FROM MANAGED FORESTS

Concerned that your lumber may come from irreplaceable forests? The Forest Stewardship Council is an international organization that promotes sustainable forestry and certifies producers who meet the group's standards. Find the council onthe Internet at www.fscus.org/

All rooms use at least some molding, usually along the base of walls and around windows and doors. In those places, molding covers up gaps. Other molding protects corners from dents or protects walls from damage by chair backs. In other places, such as around mantels, along the ceiling, and where paint and wallcoverings meet in the middle of a wall, molding serves a decorative function. The molding you choose goes a long way toward defining the look of a room, whether it's minimalist or lushly decorative.

Molding is available in random lengths from 6 to 16 feet. Most is made of softwood, usually pine. Some popular types are available in hardwood, usually oak. These are a little more expensive.

The cost of molding does add up, so make a list of each piece you need, rounding the length up to the nearest foot, then add 5 percent to allow for trimming and fitting. See pages 20–26 for molding installation tips.

ALTERNATIVE MATERIALS

Finger-jointed molding is made of short pieces joined end to end. It costs less than regular molding, but is suitable only where you will paint the moldings.

Plastic molding is inexpensive but has wood-grain finishes that may not suit your style. (Some can be painted.)

If you plan to paint molding rather than stain it, you may be able to save time and money with a preprimed molding.

Paper-covered hardboard molding also costs less but can be difficult to cut neatly, and the paper may tear later.

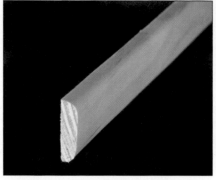

Screen bead regular

Screen bead fluted

Half round

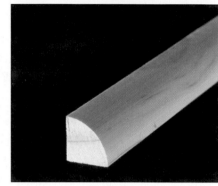

Quarter round

Inside corner

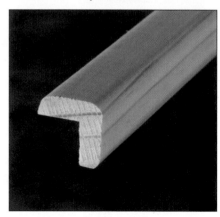

Outside corner

Base shoe

Baseboard

Ranch stop

Colonial stop

Cove molding

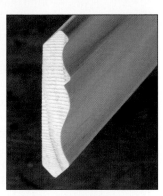

Crown molding

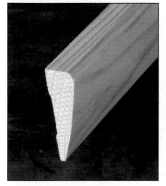

Ranch casing

Colonial casing

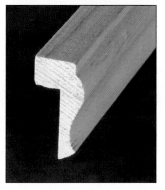

Wainscot/ply cap

Chair rail

Batten

Brick mold

MOLDING SELECTOR

Common Types	Typical Uses
Screen bead: regular and fluted	Both cover seams where screening fastens to frames; finish edges of shelves.
Half round	Serves as screen bead, shelf edging, and lattice.
Quarter round	General corner trim and inside corner guard.
Inside corner and outside corner	Both conceal seams and protect areas where walls meet at corners.
Base shoe and baseboard	Both trim and protect walls at their base.
Stop: ranch and colonial	Both attach to door jambs to limit door swing; hold inside sash of windows in place.
Cove and crown	Both trim and conceal joints between walls and ceilings.
Casing: ranch and colonial	Both trim around interior windows and doors.
Wainscot/ply cap	Conceals paneling edge; tops off wainscoting.
Chair rail	Protects walls from chair backs; hides seams where wall materials meet.
Batten	Conceals vertical and horizontal panel seams.
Brick mold	Used with all types of exterior cladding (not just brick) to trim around doors and windows.

SELECTING SHEET GOODS

Sheet goods are easy to work with and an inexpensive way to neatly cover large surface areas. For many applications, they provide the strength and appearance you need at a fraction of the cost of dimensional lumber.

Plywood is made by laminating thin layers (or plies) of wood using water-resistant glue. The plies are sandwiched, with the grain of each successive ply running at 90 degrees to the grain of the previous layer. This gives plywood its tremendous strength, as you will find if you try to break a piece in two. The front and back surface plies may be made of softwood—usually fir—or hardwood. A plywood surface rated A is smooth and free of defects; B, C, and D faces are progressively rougher. Both faces need not be graded the same, for example, A-C. T1-11 plywood siding is made with exterior adhesive and a rough veneer.

Wood particles, sawdust, and glue are compressed and bonded together by heat to form **particleboard** and **hardboard.** This process produces a material that is hard but easy to break. Hardboard comes in tempered (very hard) and untempered (softer) composition and is available in a variety of textures. Particleboard comes in a variety of densities. Particleboard laminated with a plastic surface is handy for cabinet construction. **Waferboard** is made by a similar process but with scraps of thin wood rather than sawdust, making it similar to plywood.

Drywall, sometimes called wallboard, is made of gypsum powder sandwiched between layers of heavy paper. **Cement board** is made with portland cement and fillers.

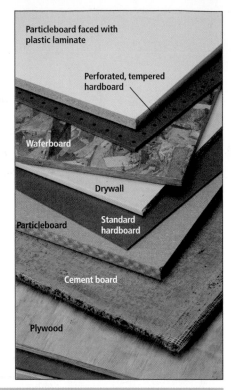

Particleboard faced with plastic laminate

Perforated, tempered hardboard

Waferboard

Drywall

Particleboard

Standard hardboard

Cement board

Plywood

SHEET GOODS SELECTOR

Material	Grades and Common Types	Thickness (in inches)	Common Panel Sizes (in feet)	Typical Uses
Plywood sheathing	C-D, C-D Exterior	⅜, ½, ⅝, ¾	4×8	Sheathing, subflooring, underlayment, structural supports. Tongue-and-groove and shiplap versions are available.
Finish plywood	A-B, A-C, B-C	¼, ⅜, ½, ⅝, ¾	4×8, 2×4	Cabinets, cabinet doors, shelves, soffits.
Hardwood plywood	A-A (or A-2), G1S (good one side); hardwood side sometimes labeled N	¼, ¾	4×8, 2×4	Cabinets, cabinet doors, shelves, wall panels.
Lauan subflooring	Only one type	¼	4×8, 2×4	Underlayment for vinyl tiles or sheet goods, backing for cabinets.
T1-11 siding	Rough, with grooves variously spaced	⅜, ½, ⅝	4×8, 4×9	Exterior siding.
Oriented strand board	Only one type	¼, ⁷⁄₁₆, ½, ¾	4×8	Roof sheathing, underlayment.
Particleboard	Density of material varies	¼, ⅜, ½, ⅝, ¾	4×8, 2×4	Underlayment, core material for laminated furniture and countertops.
Hardboard	Standard, tempered, perforated	⅛, ¼	4×8, 2×4	Underlayment, drawer bottoms and partitions, cabinet backs, tool organizers.
Drywall	Standard, water-resistant greenboard	¼, ⅜, ½, ⅝	4×8, 4×10, 4×12	Interior walls.
Cement board	Cement/clay, cement/foam	⁵⁄₁₆, ½	32"×60"	Backing for wall tiles, underlayment for ceramic floors.

HANDLING AND STORING MATERIALS

One of the joys of having your own shop is the pile of useful materials you collect over time. To ensure a safe, uneventful trip home from your home center, secure materials to your vehicle with rope, bungee cords, or twine. For large purchases or if your vehicle cannot handle the load, pay a little extra and have the materials delivered to your house.

When transporting or unloading sheet goods, have a helper on hand. If that's not possible, lift a panel with one hand near the center of each long edge, as shown in the inset *below*. Pick the panel up and rest it on your shoulder; avoid carrying it with a bent back. The exception is drywall: Because it's thin, heavy, and brittle, it can snap under its own weight. Get help with drywall. Take care not to damage the edges or scratch the surface of the sheets.

Too quickly, however, your pile of material can become a headache and an eyesore. To keep boards and sheet goods easily accessible and to prevent warping and other damage, keep these tips in mind:

■ Store materials in a cool, dry place, off the floor. Moisture can distort lumber, delaminate some plywoods, and render drywall useless. If your basement gets wet occasionally, store materials above the high-water line.

■ Ideally sheet goods should be stored flat. Because most people lack the room to do this, it's best to stand sheet goods on edge, as shown *below*, as vertical as possible to keep them from bowing.

■ Build a storage rack like the one shown *below* to keep lumber at eye level. You want to see the ends of boards clearly and be able to pull out what you need easily.

■ If you don't build a rack, store lumber flat and weigh it down at each end and in the center to prevent warping and other distortions. Weighting is especially important if the wood has a high moisture content.

1×3

1×4

Keep materials off floor; add height if moisture is likely.

Pick up sheet goods by lifting from knees, not back.

SELECTING NAILS

Many types and sizes of nails are available, each one engineered for a specific use. The differences may seem small, but they can have a significant effect on the soundness and appearance of your job. Here's a guide to choosing among the standard types of nails:

Use **common nails** and **box nails** for framing jobs. Box nails are a bit thinner for lighter work. **Cement-coated nails** drive more easily and hold more firmly. Attach drywall to framing with **drywall nails**. Use **roofing nails** for roof shingles and wherever a wide head is needed to hold material that might tear if a smaller head is used. Choose hot-dipped over electroplated **galvanized nails;** they'll last much longer.

Casing and **finishing nails** handle medium- and heavy-duty finishing work. For very fine work use **wire brads. Ringshank** and **spiral nails** grab wood more tightly than conventional nails. Specially hardened **masonry nails** penetrate mortar joints, brick, and even concrete. **Corrugated fasteners** are used mainly for strengthening wood joints; they do not hold well by themselves.

Nails are normally sold in various-size boxes. If you are planning a large project, buying a large box usually saves you some money.

THE TIP OF A NAIL

The tip of a common, box, or finishing nail is not symmetrical. Viewed point on, the tip is diamond shaped, not square, due to the way these nails are stamped. If you start the nail so the flatter side of the diamond is parallel to the grain of the board you are nailing it into, you're less likely to split the wood than if the flat side were against the grain.

PENNIES AND INCHES

In Britain in the 1400s, so one story goes, 100 medium-size nails cost 8 pennies. It didn't take long for the price to creep up, but we still use the term penny to express nail sizes. The abbreviation "d" for penny comes from denarius, a small, silver Roman coin used in Britain that equated with a penny.

Inch equivalent of nails sizes:

3d=1¼"	10d=3"
4d=1½"	12d=3¼"
6d=2"	16d=3½"
7d=2¼"	20d=4"
8d=2½"	

The nail for the job. Use nails three times as long as the thickness of the material you are fastening. For instance, to attach a 1×4 (¾ inch thick), a 6d nail (2 inches long) will be a bit short. An 8d nail (2½ inches long, a little more than three times the thickness of the 1×4) will do better. Make sure the nail will not poke through the material to which you are fastening.

Types of nails

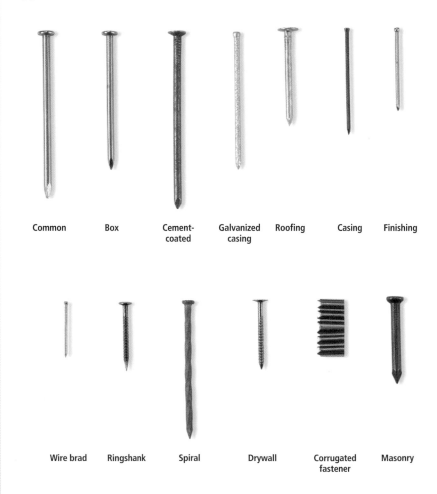

Common   Box   Cement-coated   Galvanized casing   Roofing   Casing   Finishing

Wire brad   Ringshank   Spiral   Drywall   Corrugated fastener   Masonry

For the few seconds they take to drive, nails do a remarkable holding job. Yet for the little extra time it takes to drive a screw, you get a tighter-holding fastener, a neater appearance, and another plus—ease of disassembly. In fact, drywall screws teamed with cordless electric drills have created a mini-revolution in fasteners, including everything from **deck screws** to general-purpose **wood screws.**

The most common slot configurations for screws are the **slotted head** and the **phillips head,** which has an X-shaped slot. Square-drive screws are more rare but are growing in popularity.

There are three head shapes from which to choose. A **flathead screw** can be driven flush with or slightly below the surface of the wood. Use **ovalhead screws** with **trim washers** for a finished appearance. Install **roundhead screws** when you want the screw head to show.

General-purpose or **drywall screws** offer an inexpensive and easy way to fasten items together. You can buy them by the pound, and they drive easily using a drill with a screwdriver bit. **Trim-head screws** use a smaller phillips or square-drive bit. They hold better than finishing nails, but the countersunk hole will be larger.

Use **masonry screws** (often referred to by the brand name Tap-Con) to fasten material to masonry or concrete surfaces. Simply drill the correct-size hole in the masonry surface and drive the screw. Drive a **hanger screw** into a ceiling joist and fasten the object to be hung using the nut and thread on the screw's lower half.

Use **lag screws** for heavy-duty fastening. Drill a pilot hole and drive the screw with a wrench. Thin metal can be joined with self-tapping **sheet-metal screws.**

As with nails, screws should be three times as long as the thickness of the board being fastened. When buying screws, specify the gauge (diameter) you want. The thicker the gauge, the greater its holding power. Make sure you have the correct-size drill bit if drilling pilot holes (see the box at *right*). For more on driving screws, see pages 133–134.

Machine bolts have a head that can be turned with a wrench. **Carriage bolts** have round heads for a finished appearance. When buying bolts, be sure to get the correct diameter and length; the bolt must be longer than the materials you are fastening so you can add the nut and **washers.** (For more on fastening with bolts, see page 56.)

(For more on fastening with bolts, see page 56.)

DRILLING PILOT HOLES

To see if a drill bit is the correct size for a pilot hole, grip both bit and screw together with your fingers. The bit should be slightly thinner than the width of the screw threads.

The thickness of a pilot hole can vary depending on the wood. With softwoods you can use a smaller hole than you would with hardwoods. Always drill a test hole and make sure the screw will hold tight before you proceed to drill a number of holes in the finished material.

ADHESIVES

Many jobs call for adhesives, either as the primary or secondary fastener. Purchase a supply of wood glue for general-purpose work, construction adhesive in tubes, two-part epoxy glue for extra-strong holding, panel adhesive for installing drywall or paneling, and perhaps a hot-glue gun with glue sticks.

Wood screw · Flat-head screw · Roundhead screw · Ovalhead screw · Slotted-head screw · Phillips-head screw · Lock washer · Sheet-metal screw · Flat washer · Trim washer · Lag screw · Hanger screw · Machine bolt · Carriage bolt · Deck screw · Drywall screw · Trim-head screw · Masonry (Tap-Con) screw

SELECTING HARDWARE

The items shown on these two pages represent just a few of the options available in specialized hardware. At your hardware store or home center, you'll find a product designed for almost every conceivable carpentry need.

When you want to strengthen a wood joint, add a metal plate or brace, as shown *below*. **Mending plates** reinforce end-to-end joints; **T-plates** handle end-to-edge joints. **Flat corner irons** strengthen corner joints by attaching to the face of the material; **angle brackets** do the same thing, but attach to the inside or outside edges.

Shelf standards, as shown *below*, come in a variety of configurations and finishes suitable for utilitarian or more decorative purposes. Most standards can be installed on the wall or into supports behind the shelves. Some standards can be installed on either side of the shelves. **Adjustable standards and brackets** come in a variety of colors, sizes, and finishes. Use **utility brackets** for nonadjustable shelving in places where appearance is not important. **Closet rod brackets** let you attach a shelf and a closet rod to the same piece of hardware.

A large choice of door and cabinet hardware is available, as shown on page 103. Most full-size doors hang on the classic **butt hinge** (see page 46). For extra household security, add a **chain lock** to your door. **Piano hinges** mount flush on cabinets and chests, combining great strength with a slim, finished look. **Strap hinges** and **T-hinges** often are used on gates and trunk lids.

Cabinet hinges are available in four basic types. **Decorative hinges** work only for doors that are flush with the frame. Use **front-** or **side-mount offset hinges** for doors that are flush with the frame or that have lips that overlay the frame. If a door completely overlays the frame, use a **pivot hinge** or a self-closing **European-style hidden hinge.** To open your cabinet doors, fit them with **knobs** or **pulls,** available in a myriad of sizes and styles. **Friction, roller, bullet,** or **magnetic catches** keep cabinet doors closed. (If you are using self-closing hinges, catches aren't necessary.)

For smooth-operating drawers, choose side-mounted **drawer slides** like the one shown on page 103.

SELECT APPROPRIATE JOINT REINFORCEMENT.

For a quick and fairly permanent joint or repair, use inexpensive plates like these. Clamp the material together before attaching the plates. Drill pilot holes as centered as possible; otherwise, screws may pull the joint apart as they are driven.

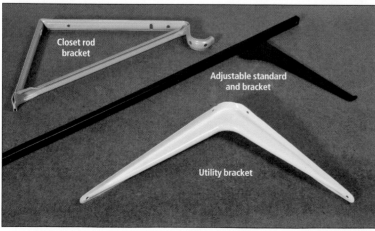

CHOOSE FROM MANY SHELF BRACKETS.

If you've ever tried to make a shelf bracket out of lumber, you'll realize how much time and effort is saved by using these handy pieces of hardware. For more on installing shelf hardware and shelf construction, see pages 38–41.

Door, gate and bench hardware

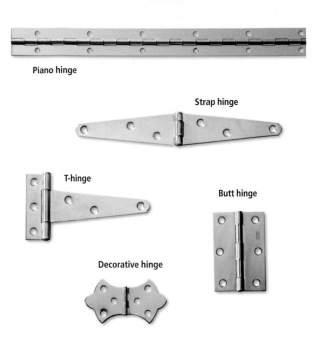

Piano hinge

Strap hinge

T-hinge

Butt hinge

Decorative hinge

Cabinet hardware

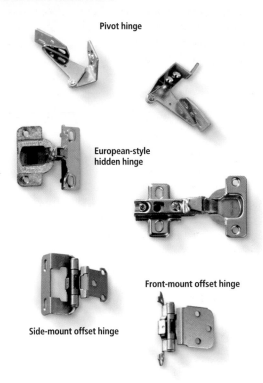

Pivot hinge

European-style hidden hinge

Front-mount offset hinge

Side-mount offset hinge

Latch, lock and handle hardware

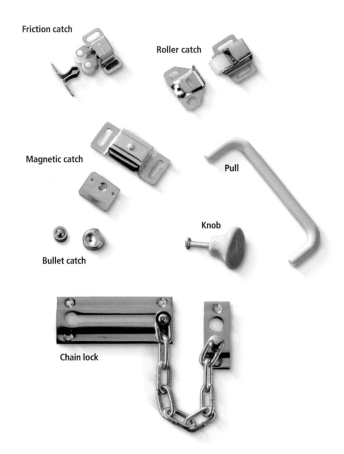

Friction catch

Roller catch

Magnetic catch

Pull

Bullet catch

Knob

Chain lock

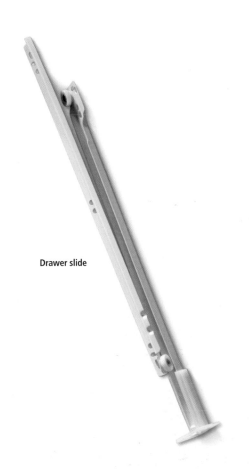

Drawer slide

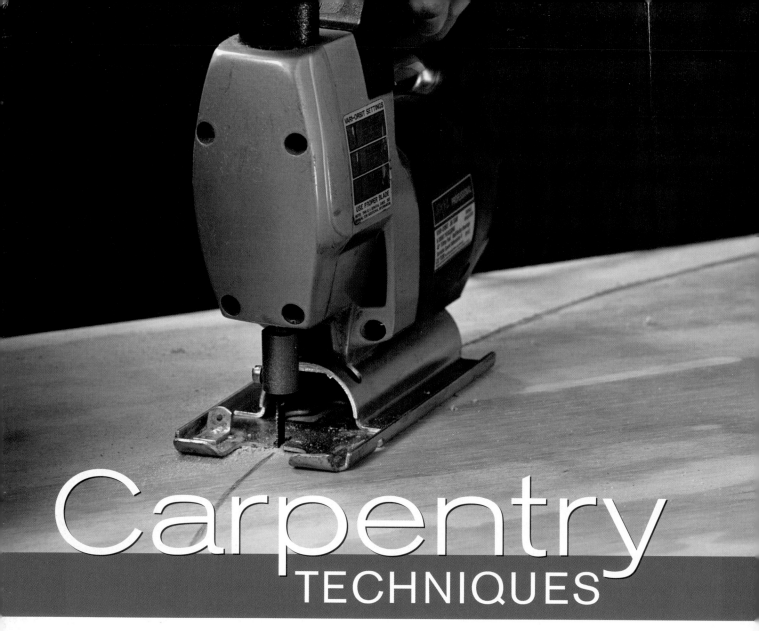

Carpentry
TECHNIQUES

The first time you picked up a hammer, you might have wondered if you could avoid hitting your thumb. Questioning capabilities is natural, especially if the result is pain. But you ardently drove that nail and avoided doing too much damage to yourself or anything else. The next time, you became more comfortable and adept with the hammer. With each use, you improved until you were driving nails like a pro and mastering techniques.

Carpentry is all about technique. Mastering technique requires practice. Before diving into a project where new skills are required, practice a couple of times on scrap. Just as you wouldn't expect to pick up a musical instrument and play an acceptable melody, you shouldn't expect to barge through a project without the proper skills and still have a beautiful result.

This section prepares you by giving examples of how to use equipment and materials. You'll begin by learning measuring techniques. Learn how to properly use hand and power tools. You'll understand the process of fastening materials. The last portion tells you how to shape, plane, sand, file, and properly finish your project. Once you understand the techniques of carpentry, you're ready to begin. Now go build something and have fun!

PERFECT A TECHNIQUE

Several basic techniques are the basis for almost any carpentry project or repair. Spending a few minutes reviewing those techniques may make projects go faster and improve the end results.

CUT PRECISELY

Installing elaborate crown molding such as this involves precise cuts with a miter box (see page 116) as well as other basic carpentry techniques—such as holding and measuring in place—found in this chapter. After a review of the skills involved and some practice, you'll be ready to undertake projects that will transform your home.

INSTALL A SHELF

Display shelves can make a dramatic decorating statement. Making these striking shelves requires only a few basic carpentry skills including marking and cutting techniques described in this chapter. Turn to page 42 for instructions on building the decorative molding shelves.

MEASURING AND MARKING

Accurate measuring and marking are essential to successful carpentry. A mistake in measuring often means wasted time and material. Though it may seem simple, good measuring technique takes practice.

Don't rush your measuring. Take your time and double-check your work. Adopt the carpenters' maxim, "Measure twice, cut once."

No matter what measuring device you use, get comfortable with it and learn how to read it accurately. Many a board has met its ruin because someone couldn't distinguish a ¼-inch mark from a ⅛-inch mark. Once you've made a measurement, don't trust your memory. Jot down the figure on a piece of paper or a wood scrap. The best practice is to use the same measuring device for all measurements whenever possible. A poor fit could result if you measure the width of a window for a piece of molding with a yardstick, then measure the molding itself with a tape measure, for example.

Often marking, not reading, the measurement introduces error. Make a clear mark (see the opposite page) using a sharp No. 2 pencil, the thin edge of a sharpened carpenter's pencil, a knife, or a scratch awl.

COMPARE MEASURING DEVICES

Odd as it may seem, different measuring tapes or rulers can differ slightly, and the discrepancies will show up when dealing with long spans of lumber. This can lead to frustration if you are calling out measurements for someone else to cut. Before you accuse your partner of sloppy cutting, compare measuring devices to be sure they're calibrated the same.

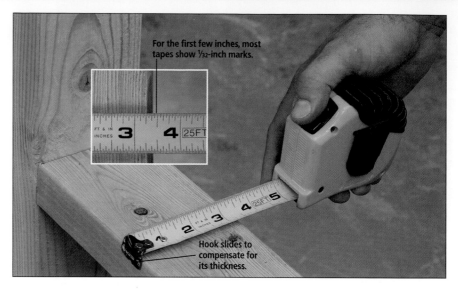

For the first few inches, most tapes show 1/32-inch marks.

Hook slides to compensate for its thickness.

MEASURE WITH A STEEL TAPE.

A steel tape is the most popular measuring device because it does most jobs with ease. Note that the hook at the end of the tape slides back and forth slightly to compensate for its own thickness. This means that whether you hook the tape on a board end for an outside measurement or push it against a surface for an inside measurement, the result will be accurate. For the first few inches of most tapes, each inch is divided into 1/32-inch increments to facilitate extra-fine measurements.

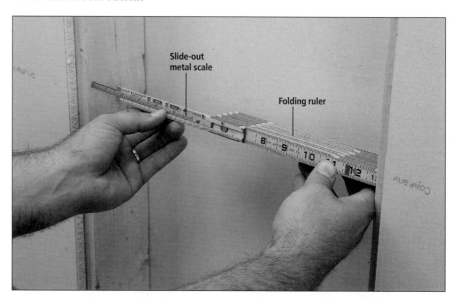

Slide-out metal scale

Folding ruler

TAKE AN INSIDE MEASUREMENT.

Where outside measurement is difficult (here the drywall is in the way of measuring between the outside edges of the 2×4s), make an inside-to-inside measurement. A folding ruler with a slide-out metal scale works best. Extend it, measure, and hold the slide with your thumb until the measurement is transferred. You can use a tape measure for such measurements, but it is difficult to be accurate because you have to add an amount to compensate for the length of the tape body.

Mark a V.

Slide the square to the mark.

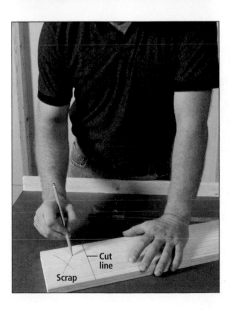

Cut line

Scrap

Pull straight up and let go.

Mark a double line to allow for saw kerf.

MAKE A V MARK, NOT A LINE.

Marking with a simple line often leads to inaccuracies. By the time you're ready to saw, it's easy to forget which end of the line marks the spot—or where to cut on a thick line from a blunt pencil. For greater accuracy, mark your measurements with a V so you know precisely where to strike the cut line. To ensure pinpoint accuracy, place the point of your pencil at the V, slide the square to it, then make your line.

If you need to extend cut lines across several boards, use a framing square. For longer lines, use a drywall square.

MARK FOR RIP CUTS.

Need to mark a cutoff line along the length of a board or a piece of plywood? If the line is parallel to the edge of the board and accuracy isn't critical, use your tape measure as a scribing device. Hold your tape so that a pencil laid against its end will make the correct line. Hold the tape and pencil firmly and pull evenly toward you, letting the tape body or your thumbnail slide along the board edge. For sheet goods, first mark the cutoff line at both ends, then snap a chalk line between the two marks, or clamp a straightedge in place and draw a mark.

ALLOW FOR THE SAW KERF.

When you cut material, the saw blade reduces some of it to sawdust. So when measuring, you must allow for the wood removed by the blade—called the kerf. Usually a kerf is about ⅛ inch wide. If you're making just one cut, account for the kerf by marking the waste side of the cutoff line with an X. This avoids confusion as to the side of the line on which to cut.

If you are cutting multiple pieces out of the same piece of lumber, make double marks to allow for the kerf.

The most accurate and mistake-proof way of measuring is not to use a measuring device at all. Simply hold a piece where it needs to fit and mark it. You can do this for a simple cutoff. At other times, such as when you need to cut a board in two directions, use a combination of techniques: Hold and mark, then measure. Often this method isn't feasible, especially where access is limited or when the lumber being cut is too bulky to be held in place. But take advantage of this foolproof approach when you can.

NO-MISTAKE MEASURING

Carpenters make measuring mistakes every day, so don't be surprised when you do also. Here are some common mistakes and how to avoid them:

- Sawing on the wrong side of the line. If you cut on the good rather than the scrap side of the line, the board will be about ⅛ inch short. Always draw an X on the scrap side (see page 107).

- Misreading upside-down numbers. Is it a 6 or a 9? Make sure you know.

- Simply forgetting. Write down all measurements immediately so you won't forget.

YOU'LL NEED

TIME: Less than 1 minute for most measurements.

SKILLS: A steady hand, a good eye for accurate marking.

TOOLS: Pencil, speed square.

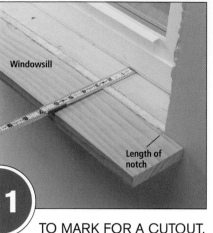

1 TO MARK FOR A CUTOUT, FIRST MEASURE THE DEPTH OF THE CUT.

When you need to cut a board in two or three directions to make it fit around something, begin by holding the board in place. Make a small mark showing where the cutout is to be cut to length. Then measure how deep the cutout must be by measuring the distance between the leading edge of the board and the place where it must end up once it's cut.

HOLD AND MARK FOR A CUTOFF.

When you need to cut a board to length, begin by checking one end of the board for square. Press the square-cut end against one side of the opening and mark the other end for cutting. To avoid distorting the measurement, don't push the square-cut end into the space any more than needed.

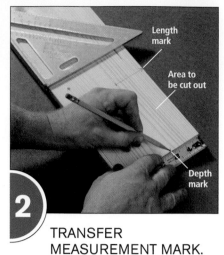

2 TRANSFER MEASUREMENT MARK.

Use a square to extend the length mark. With a tape measure, transfer the depth measurement to two places on the board—at the length mark and at the end of the cutout. Use a square to draw a line from the length mark to the depth mark. With a straightedge, mark a line between the two depth marks.

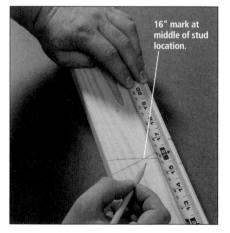

LAY OUT A PLATE FOR A STUD WALL.

When building a wall, the studs (upright 2×4s) must be 16 inches on center; that is, you want 48- or 96-inch drywall or paneling sheets to end in the middle of a stud. To make marks for studs, mark every 16 inches, minus ¾ inch (15¼ inches, 31¼ inches, and so on). Measure over 1½ inches and make another mark. Draw lines at your marks and an X between to show stud location (see page 51).

SQUARING, PLUMBING, AND LEVELING

Most carpentry projects—from making simple shelves to building walls—require that you square the work. Check for square at every stage of your work: corners, uprights, and board ends.

Making sure that work is plumb and level is equally important. Walls, cabinets, doors—nearly every permanent installation—must be plumb (perpendicular to the earth) and level (parallel to the earth). Don't assume existing walls or floors are square, level, or plumb. Most often they are not because of imperfect construction or settling that has taken place over the years. Techniques shown in this section will help you keep your carpentry projects straight and true.

YOU'LL NEED

TIME: Two minutes or less to check that work is square, plumb, or level.

SKILLS: Using squares and levels.

TOOLS: Combination, speed, and framing squares; 2- or 4-foot level; other levels.

CHECK BOARD ENDS FOR SQUARE.

All your careful measuring will be wasted if you start with a piece of lumber that is not square—one edge will be longer than the other. Check the board end by holding a combination square with the body or handle firmly against a factory edge. If the end isn't square, mark a square line and trim the board.

USE A COMBINATION SQUARE.

With this tool you can easily check for either 45- or 90-degree angles. Also, by sliding the blade, you can check depths. This tool can go out of square if it is dropped, so check it once in a while against a square factory edge (such as the corner of a sheet of plywood).

USE A FRAMING SQUARE.

For larger jobs, use a framing square. Lay the square up against two members where they meet. If the tongue and the blade of the square rest neatly against the members, the sides are square. Or place the square on the outside. Again, if the square touches the members at all points, the unit is square. When using a framing square for measuring, be sure to read the correct scale—inside or outside.

Squaring, plumbing, and leveling *(continued)*

USE THE 3-4-5 METHOD.

For large projects, test if a corner is square by using geometry. You don't need to remember the Pythagorean theorem, just remember "3-4-5." On one side, mark a point 3 feet from the corner. On the other side, mark a point 4 feet from the corner. If the distance between the two marks is exactly 5 feet, the corner is square.

For extra large projects, use multiples such as 6-8-10 or 9-12-15.

As a doublecheck, measure the length of the diagonals. If the project is square, the distance between two opposite corners (marked A in the drawing above) will equal the distance between the other two corners (B).

First mark and fasten here.

Then level cleat and fasten here.

CHECK FOR PLUMB.

To see if a piece is plumb (perfectly vertical), hold a level against one face of the vertical surface and look at the bubble in the level's lower glass vial. If it rests between the two guide marks, the piece is plumb.

CHECK FOR LEVEL.

In most cases, you can simply set your carpenter's level on a piece to see if it's level. Raise or lower the piece until the bubble rests between the marks. Mark the position of the piece and remove the level (you don't want to risk knocking it to the floor). Add a fastener to the cleat near the level mark, level the cleat, and finish fastening.

TEST FOR LEVEL OVER LONG DISTANCES WITH A BOARD...

If you need to see if an entire floor is level, select a long, straight board. (Sight down its length to see that it's not bowed.) Place a carpenter's level in the center of the board and raise one end or the other until the bubble is centered between the two lines. Slide the board around until you are sure you have found the high point of the floor. Level the board from this point and measure the distance from the floor to the bottom of the raised end of the board to see how far out of level the floor is.

OR USE A WATER LEVEL.

This tool enables you to quickly check for level in awkward situations or over long distances. Basically a long hose and two transparent tubes filled with water, this tool works on the principle that water seeks its own level. Mark at water level.

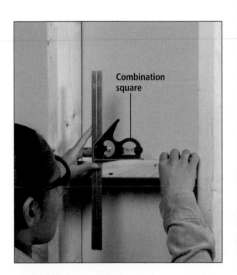

USE SMALL LEVELS IN TIGHT SPOTS.

In places where you can't fit a carpenter's level, use the level that comes on some combination squares or a torpedo level (a short version of a carpenter's level). Or, if you know that an adjoining member or wall is plumb, check that the piece is square to it.

PLUMB A CABINET.

When installing cabinets, make sure they are plumb in both directions or the doors will shut or open by themselves. With the cabinet fastened loosely to the wall, hold a level against a vertical framing piece. Tap in shims until the bubble indicates that the cabinet is plumb.

TEST YOUR LEVEL

Test a new level for accuracy before buying it. If the first one you try isn't accurate, the next one on the shelf may be. If you own a level, test it to see if it has been knocked out of alignment.

To make sure your level is accurate, set it on a shelf or table and note the location of the bubble. Then turn the level around end for end on the same surface. It should give exactly the same reading.

If it is not accurate, you may be able to adjust it by loosening the four small screws holding the bubble assembly and turning the assembly until it is correct. If the level isn't adjustable, you'll have to buy a new one.

A flexible steel tape measure, a square, and a level usually will equip you to mark your lumber for cutting. But sometimes you'll come across a situation where you'll have to mark around the irregular contours of molding, brick, or stone; mark curved shapes; or mark for angles other than 45 and 90 degrees. The simple techniques in this section are for marking unusual shapes.

MAKING AND USING TEMPLATES

For material in which you are making multiple or complicated cuts, make a template or pattern before you make the cut. Often the piece of lumber or sheet goods you are replacing can serve as the template. Carefully remove the old piece, take out any nails or screws that are in it, place it over the new lumber, and trace its outline.

At other times, you may need to make a template. Cut a piece of stiff cardboard with a knife or make a pattern out of a piece of scrap wood. Experiment until the template fits exactly (without experimenting on your final, expensive materials).

Whenever you use a template, be sure that it does not slide around as you make your marks—you may need to clamp or tack it in place. Watch your pencil line carefully to see that it is tight against the template at all points.

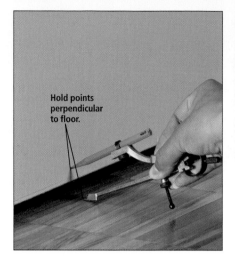

Hold points perpendicular to floor.

SCRIBE A DOOR BOTTOM.

If the bottom of a door is sticking, close it as far as possible. Set a compass to the correct height above the floor—usually the thickness of the threshold plus ⅛ inch for clearance. Hold the compass point on the floor and the pencil end of the compass on the door. Move the compass along the floor, scribing a cutoff line on the door.

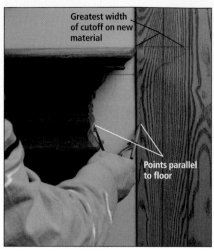

Greatest width of cutoff on new material

Points parallel to floor

MARK FOR IRREGULAR CUTS.

For a complicated contour cut, use a compass that can be tightened firmly so it won't collapse or expand as you trace the contour. Place the new material next to the object it will fit around. Set the compass to the greatest width to be cut off. Take care to hold the two compass points on the same plane (in this case, parallel to the floor) as you make the mark.

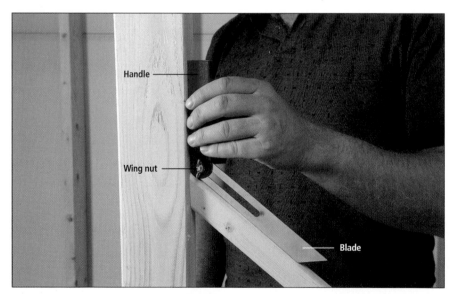

Handle

Wing nut

Blade

USE A T-BEVEL FOR ODD ANGLES.

If you want to duplicate an angle that is neither 45 nor 90 degrees, use a sliding T-bevel. Loosen the wing nut so you can move the blade without difficulty. Hold the handle against one edge and move the blade until it rests firmly against the other edge. Tighten the wing nut firmly. The tool holds the angle you need, allowing you to transfer it to the wood you are cutting. When making an inside measurement, as shown *above*, extend the blade fully to ensure an accurate reading.

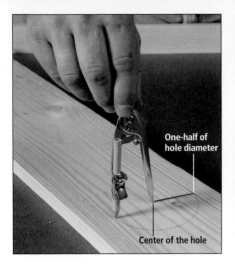

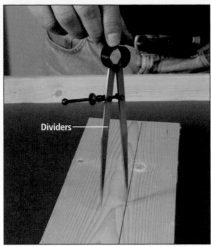

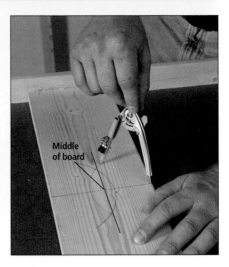

DRAW SMALL CIRCLES.

To mark small circles—for boards that will be cut to accept pipes, lighting fixtures, etc.—a simple compass will do the job. Mark a spot at the center of the hole and set the compass width to one-half the diameter of the hole. For accuracy, be sure the compass is tightly clamped in position and hold it as perpendicular to the surface as possible.

STEP OFF WITH DIVIDERS.

If you need to mark a series of equidistant points along a straight line, use dividers. Steel pins at the base of each leg grip the surface of the material you're measuring for good control. Use a swiveling motion as you step from one leg to the other leg.

FIND THE MIDDLE.

If you need to find the middle of a board, doing it using math can be confusing—what's half of $9\frac{1}{4}$ inches, for instance? To quickly find the middle, open your compass to a bit more than half the board's width and make two arcing marks as shown. The line between the points where the curved lines intersect is the middle of the board.

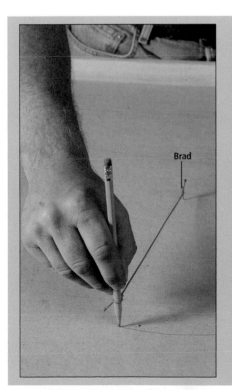

DRAW LARGER CIRCLES.

A compass works well for small circles, but if you have to cut out for a sink or another large round object, you will have to use a little ingenuity. Make your own compass out of a pencil, brad, and string. Be sure to hold the pencil vertically as you draw.

For greater accuracy, make a notch at one end of a small piece of wood. Nail the wood piece in place with a brad at the center of the circle. The notch holds the pencil in place for a smooth, accurate line.

Sometimes you may be able to find a round household object, such as a can, a bucket, or a wastebasket, that is close enough to the correct size. Place it on the work and trace around it.

Chances are you will do most of your cutting with a circular saw. Whether crosscutting 1× stock, ripping plywood, or cutting bricks with a masonry blade, you'll do the job better if you follow a few basic rules when using this versatile tool.

Whenever you cut, allow the saw to reach full operating speed, then slowly push the blade into the wood. Some carpenters look at the blade as they cut; others rely on the gunsight notch. Choose the method that suits you best. Avoid making slight turns as you cut. Instead find the right path and push the saw through the material smoothly. It will take some practice before you can do this consistently. This is a powerful tool with sharp teeth, so take care. It demands your respect.

SUPPORT THE MATERIAL.

Well-supported work results in clean, safe cuts. If the scrap piece is short, support the board on the nonscrap side. If the scrap is long, it could bind the blade or splinter as it falls away at the end of the cut. To achieve a neat cut and avoid saw kickback, support the lumber in four places. Even with such precautions, you may want to make two cuts: one to cut the work roughly to size, the other for the finish cut.

CHOOSING A CIRCULAR SAW AND BLADES

Choose a circular saw that is comfortable. It should have some heft but should not be so heavy that it is difficult to maneuver. You should be able to see the blade and gunsight notch easily. Check for ease of depth and angle adjustments. (For more tips, see page 85.)

If you buy only one blade for a circular saw, choose a carbide-tipped combination blade that has at least 24 teeth. It works well for rough work and makes cuts clean enough for most finish work. For fine work, buy a plywood blade or a hollow-ground planer blade. For extensive remodeling jobs, get a second carbide-tipped blade that you can use when you may need to cut through nails or other rough materials.

CAUTION

AVOIDING AND PREPARING FOR KICKBACK

It happens to even the most experienced carpenter: A blade binds, causing a circular saw to jump backward. Kickback can mar the lumber you are working on, and it is dangerous. Unsupported work often is the culprit, but also watch for these situations:

A dull blade will bind and cause the saw to kick. Change your blade or have it sharpened if you have to push hard to make it cut.

Bending or twisting lumber will grab a blade. Sheets of plywood are particularly prone to this. Make sure it is evenly supported as the 1× above is.

Kickback also can occur when you back up while cutting or when you try to make a turn. If your cut is going off line, stop the saw, back up, and start again.

Occasionally certain types of wood grain will grab the blade and cause kickback. There's nothing you can do about this except be prepared.

Don't wear long sleeves and don't position your face near the saw.

SQUARE THE BLADE.

To square a blade, unplug the saw, hold a speed square against the blade and the base, and adjust the blade. (Be sure to position the square between the teeth.) To test if your blade is square to the baseplate, crosscut a piece of 2× lumber. Flip one piece over and press the cut ends together. If you see a gap at the top or the bottom, the blade is not square.

ALIGN THE BLADE WITH THE CUT LINE.

Once you have drawn an accurate cutoff line and have properly supported the board, position the saw blade on the scrap side of the line. The teeth on most circular saw blades are offset in an alternating pattern, half to the left and half to the right. When clamping a guide, align a tooth that points toward the cutoff line.

USE A SQUARE AS A GUIDE.

With practice, you will learn to cut accurately without using a guide. But for cuts that have to be precise, use a guide. For 90-degree cuts, a speed square works well because it's easy to hold stable. Align the blade, then slide the square into position against the saw's baseplate. Grab the board along with the square so the square will stay in position.

USE OTHER GUIDES FOR ANGLE CUTS.

With care, you can improvise a saw guide that will be as accurate as a miter box. Set a T-bevel to the desired angle (see page 112) and transfer the angle to the board.

Select a straight piece of 1× and clamp it parallel to the cut line as a saw guide. To offset the guide correctly, measure the distance between the blade and the edge of the saw's baseplate and clamp the guide

that distance from the cut line. It may take some experimenting before you get this correct. Be sure to align the blade on the correct side of the line.

You can use the same principle for long rip cuts. Clamp a straightedge—the factory edge of a 1× works well—onto the material, setting it back from the cut line to allow for the width of the saw's baseplate.

Cutting with a circular saw *(continued)*

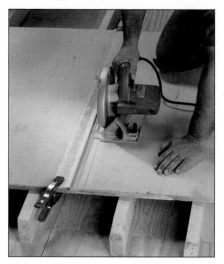

SUPPORT SHEET GOODS.

Cut sheet goods with a carbide-tipped combination blade or a plywood-cutting blade for a smoother cut. It is important to support the sheet properly, or the blade will bind. You can do this by setting four 2× support pieces on the floor, a table, or a pair of sawhorses. Arrange two support pieces on either side of the cut line so that when the cut is complete, both pieces of the sheet are stable.

USE A GUIDE.

Use a guide to make a long straight cut. Get a straightedge that is as long as the material you are cutting—a straight 1×4 or the factory edge of a piece of plywood. Measure the distance from the edge of the saw's baseplate to the blade and clamp the guide that distance from the cut line. Set the saw in place and check alignment with the cut line. Clamp the opposite end of the guide the same distance from the edge.

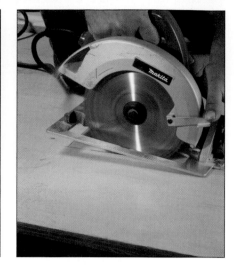

MAKE A PLUNGE CUT.

Use a plunge cut, also called a pocket cut, to make a hole or slit in the middle of a board or sheet. Set the blade to the correct depth. Retract the safety guard and tilt the saw forward, setting the front of the baseplate on your work. Start the saw and lower it slowly into the cut line until the base rests on the stock. Complete the cut.

Because you will be exposing the blade, any twist could result in dangerous kickback. Be careful.

MAKING MITER CUTS

A miter joint is made when two pieces of wood are angle-cut or bevel-cut at the same angle then joined to form a corner. Most often two pieces that have been cut at 45 degrees are joined to make a 90-degree corner. Miter cuts must be precise. If they are off even one degree, the corner will be noticeably out of true.

The most inexpensive way to make angle or bevel cuts in narrow stock is to use a miter box—essentially a jig for holding the saw at the proper angle to the work. If you have numerous miter cuts to make, consider buying a power mitersaw (see page 117).

Before placing the stock in the miter box, support it on a scrap of 1×4 or some other suitable material. This allows you to saw completely through the work without marring the bottom of the miter box. Place the member against the far side of the miter box, positioned as it will be when in use, and make the cut with a backsaw. Hold the work firmly against the back of the box with your free hand.

If there's any trick to using a miter box, it's in correctly measuring and marking for the cut rather than the cutting technique. Whenever possible, make your miter cut first, then cut the other end of the piece to the proper length with a straight cut.

MITER BOX IS A SAW GUIDE.

A miter box is essentially a jig holding a saw at the proper angle.

POWER SAW SAVES TIME.

If you have a number of cuts to make, consider renting or buying a power mitersaw. A sliding compound mitersaw offers the most versatility.

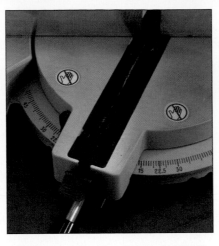

SCALE SHOWS MITER ANGLE.

The scale on the front of the mitersaw is calibrated. The center setting is 0 degrees, allowing you to make a 90-degree cut. The numbers increase on the left and right, allowing cuts of other angles. The most common cut settings for trimwork will be made with the 0- and 45-degree settings.

INSTALL BLADE ON ARBOR.

Unplug the saw and make sure the blade is properly set before operating. Mount the blade on the arbor. Tighten the blade bolt with the wrench provided by the manufacturer. The blade teeth point down and back toward the fence.

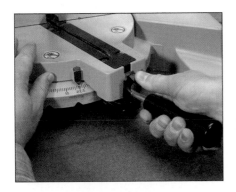

SET ANGLE ON SCALE.

To set the angle, unlock the handle, move it to the desired setting, and relock it.

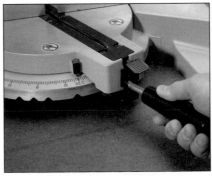

LOCK SETTING FOR CUT.

Once at the desired cut setting, lock the saw in place by turning the handle clockwise.

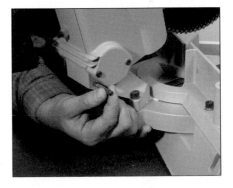

UNLOCK SAFETY PIN.

Manufacturers install a pin to lock the head down for transportation and to help prevent unintentional operation of the mitersaw. Your manual will help you locate a spring-loaded locking button. You will need to release the button to operate the saw.

OPERATE SAFELY

Mitersaws can be dangerous if used improperly. Follow these steps to ensure safe operation:

- Read the manufacturer's manual carefully. Make sure you fully understand the instructions before attempting to operate the saw. If you are unsure of yourself, ask the salesperson to demonstrate proper usage.
- Wear safety glasses or a face shield for protection from flying wood chips. If the work produces excess dust, wear a dust mask.
- Power saws generate a lot of noise. Wear proper hearing protection.
- Keep guards in place and in proper working order. Don't operate a saw without a guard.
- Wait for the motor to reach full speed before you begin cutting.

CUTTING WITH A HANDSAW

Although power tools make accurate cutting simple, sometimes a handsaw is more convenient. Learn the proper technique, and hand-cutting may turn out to be easier than you expected.

MAKE A CROSSCUT WITH A HANDSAW.

To make a crosscut with a handsaw in narrow goods, set the blade's heel end (nearest the handle) at a 45-degree angle to the work. Set the teeth on the scrap side of the cut line. To make sure the blade doesn't wander, use your thumbnail as a guide. Pull the saw back toward you several times to start the cut. Don't force the blade; use the weight of the saw to start the cut while you guide it. Saw with a rocking motion, using a steeper angle at the beginning of the downstroke and a flatter angle at its completion. Again, don't force it; let the saw do the work.

FINISH THE CUT CLEANLY.

When you near the end of the cut, support the scrap end of the piece of wood. Grasp it firmly with your free hand, exerting a slight upward pressure to keep it from binding. This also will keep the piece from snapping and splintering on the last stroke.

MAKE A CUTOUT.

To notch the corner of a board, position the blade of the saw so it is perpendicular to the work as you near the end of each cut. That way, the bottom of the board is cut the same distance as the top. Often it is helpful to reverse the position of the saw, as shown *above*.

MAKING INSIDE AND CONTOUR CUTS

Often you need to make a cut in the center of a piece of lumber or sheet goods or make a curved or irregularly shaped cut. These cuts require two basic steps. First you need to drill or plunge-cut an access hole in the material. Then you need to use a narrow-bladed tool that can handle curved cuts to follow the contours.

To begin an inside cut, use a circular saw to make a plunge cut (see page 116). You will need a jigsaw (sometimes called a saber saw) or handsaw to finish the job. If you find it difficult to make a precise plunge cut, use a drill and jigsaw—especially if the finished work will be visible.

Note: Do not attempt to make a curved cut with a circular saw. Such a practice not only can damage your saw and saw blades, it can cause dangerous kickback.

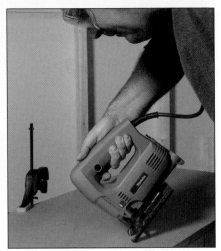

MAKE AN INSIDE CUT.

How you start an inside cut depends on the material you're cutting. With lumber and sheet goods, the safest way is to drill a starter hole at each corner of the cutout, as close as possible to the cut lines. Insert the blade of a jigsaw or keyhole saw into one of the holes and complete the cut.

If you are experienced with a jigsaw, make a plunge cut. Tip the saw forward on its baseplate, as shown. Start the saw and slowly lower the blade into the wood along the cut line. The blade tends to dance before cutting into the surface, which can badly mar your work. You may want to practice on a scrap of wood first.

CUT HOLES IN DRYWALL.

For a clean cut, score the paper face of the drywall with a knife before sawing it. Poke the tip of a drywall saw (a type of keyhole saw) into the drywall at a cut line. Either push or punch the saw handle with the heel of your hand.

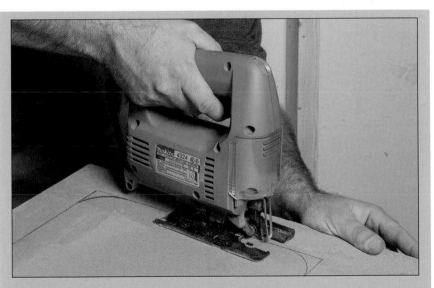

CUT CORNERS WITHOUT A PILOT HOLE.

You can maneuver a jigsaw around fairly tight corners, but don't try to make 90-degree turns. Use a three-step procedure to cut such corners. On your first approach to a corner, cut just up to the intersecting line. Carefully back the saw up about 2 inches and cut a gentle curve over to the next cut line. Continue in this direction, supporting the scrap material as you cut, until the scrap piece is free. Then go back and finish trimming the corners with short, straight cuts.

Making inside and contour cuts *(continued)*

CUT CURVES WITH A JIGSAW.

For most contour cuts, use a jigsaw. Once you get the knack of using this tool, you can cut curves that are as smooth as any line you can draw. Be sure the piece you are going to cut is stable; clamp it if necessary. Check that nothing underneath the piece you are cutting is blocking the path of the blade.

Turn the saw on, then begin the cut. Guide the saw slowly, without forcing the blade. One sharp turn can break a blade. If the saw begins to bog down or overheat, you're cutting too fast. If you wander from the line, don't try to make a correction with a sharp turn. Instead back up and start again. Support the scrap material as you reach the end of each cut to prevent it from breaking off.

USE A COPING SAW FOR FINE WORK.

For intricate cutting or scrollwork, use a coping saw. This hand tool allows you to set the blade in any direction in relation to its frame. To begin a cut from the inside of a board, remove the blade from the saw frame and reinstall it through a starter hole. For delicate cuts, install the blade with the straight faces of the teeth facing the handle so the saw cuts on the back stroke.

COPING CUTS MAKE MOLDINGS MEET.

When you're working with moldings, it's difficult to get perfectly matched miter cuts for inside corners, especially because the corners of walls often are not square. That's why professionals usually cope inside corner joints.

Start by cutting the first piece of molding at a 90-degree angle so it butts against the adjacent wall. To cope the overlapping piece, make an inside 45-degree miter cut, as shown. Use a coping saw to cut away the excess wood along the molding profile. Back-cut slightly (cut a little more off the back of the piece than the front) to ensure a neat fit. Whenever possible, make the coped cut first, hold the piece in place, then mark for the cut on the other end.

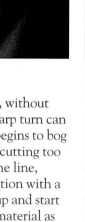

Making coped cut.

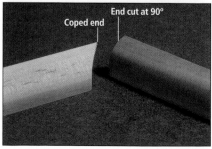

Coped end

End cut at 90°

USING CHISELS

Although you may not use a chisel every day, it pays to keep a couple of them on hand. Nothing can replace a chisel for making mortises, dadoes, or notches. An old one often comes in handy for demolition jobs.

Whenever you pick up a chisel, keep both hands behind the cutting face of the blade. As you work, point the chisel away from your body. Because it takes two hands to operate a chisel, always clamp or anchor your material. Save yourself wasted effort and ruined materials by keeping your chisels sharp. A properly sharpened chisel should slice through paper easily.

SHARPENING NICKED OR BADLY WORN TOOLS

To sharpen a nicked or badly worn chisel, a single-cut file or a bench grinder works better than a whetstone.

To sharpen a chisel with a file, clamp the chisel tightly in a vise with the cutting edge pointing up. Remove nicks by filing nearly perpendicular to the chisel edge. Then hold the file at the same angle as the chisel bevel and file diagonally across the bevel. Work slowly and evenly to obtain a sharp edge. Remove burrs on the flat side with an oiled whetstone.

To remove nicks from a chisel's blade with a bench grinder, hold the chisel nearly perpendicular to the wheel and grind until the nicks disappear. Regrind the bevel, using the guide on the grinder to hold the chisel at the bevel angle. Go slowly: Never let the cutting edge blacken or get red-hot.

① TO SHARPEN WITH A WHETSTONE, GRIND THE CUTTING EDGE.

A dull chisel edge will look flat and reflect light. It also may have nicks in it. Drip a pool of oil on a whetstone. Brace the whetstone firmly on a flat surface. Hold the chisel beveled face down at an angle slightly steeper than the bevel so you are not grinding the entire beveled face. Press the blade gently and slide it along the stone.

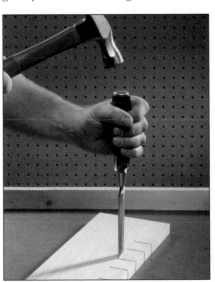

NOTCH A PIECE OF FRAMING.

Set your circular saw blade to the desired depth of the notch and make cuts at the top and bottom of the notch. If the notch is wide, make one or more cuts in the center of the notch as well. Position the chisel with the bevel facing outward. Begin cutting at a slight outward angle that gets flatter as you proceed.

② SMOOTH THE FLAT SIDE.

Turn the chisel over and lay its flat side on the whetstone. Add more oil if the stone is dry or if a thick paste has built up. Hone the flat side by pressing gently, moving the chisel with a circular motion. You don't want to grind a new cutting edge on this side; remove only the burrs created after grinding the beveled face.

MAKE A DEEP MORTISE CUT.

It is difficult to chisel deeply into a narrow board without splintering it. Begin by drilling a series of adjacent holes within the scored outline of the mortise. If possible, use a drill bit that is the same diameter as the width of the mortise. Finish the cut with a chisel, holding the beveled face toward the inside of the mortise as you gently tap.

Using chisels (continued)

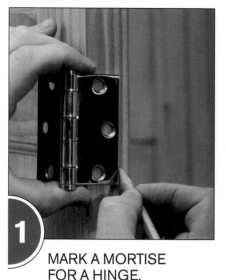

① MARK A MORTISE FOR A HINGE.

Do not attempt to layout a hinge mortise just by measuring; use the hinge itself as a template. Position it correctly on the edge of the door and mark its perimeter with a sharp pencil. (For an alternative method, see page 46.) Mark for the depth of the mortise also.

② SCORE THE LINES.

To prevent the wood grain from splintering at the edges of chisel cuts, score the lines you just marked by gently cutting with a utility knife. Once you have established the score lines, go over them again with the knife until you have cut to the depth of the mortise. A butt marker also can be used to score lines (see page 46).

③ CHISEL THE MORTISE.

Hold the chisel with the beveled face down at the angle shown. Whenever possible, cut in the direction in which the wood grain runs. Otherwise, the chisel will follow the grain deeper into the board than you intended. Drive the chisel to the depth of the mortise, making several slices across its width.

Making dadoes

① LAY OUT A DADO.

When laying out dado cuts across the width of a board, take care to draw straight, square lines that mark the exact thickness of the part that will fit into the dado. Use a framing or a smaller square to mark both the top and bottom of the cut.

② CUT LINES WITH A CIRCULAR SAW.

Adjust your circular saw blade to the correct depth—often one-third or one-half of the wood thickness. Use a speed square (see page 115) or a clamped-on guide to ensure that you stay on the outline marks. After cutting the two outside lines for wide dadoes, make a series of passes through the center of each notch.

③ CHISEL OUT THE WASTE.

Using a chisel the same width as or narrower than your dadoes, tap out the remaining slivers of wood. Start from one edge and work toward the middle, then work from the other edge. Smooth the bottom of the notch by scraping it with your chisel, flat side down.

USING A TABLESAW

When shopping for a tablesaw, use a straightedge to check the table; it should be a perfectly flat plane. If the table has extensions, make sure they are flat as well. A small, lightweight tablesaw is handy if you need to move it around often. However, the smaller table area makes it more difficult to use, and you will have a hard time making accurate cuts on large pieces.

The fence of a tablesaw should move smoothly along its guide rails and lock firmly and exactly parallel to the blade.

If possible, turn the saw on and watch the blade. There should be no hint of a wobble. A belt-driven tablesaw works more smoothly and lasts longer than one with direct drive.

1 MAKE A RIP CUT.

Check that the fence is perfectly parallel to the blade by measuring the space between the blade and the fence at the front and the rear of the blade. Set the blade depth ¼ inch above the top of the board. Start the motor and allow it to reach full speed. Hold the lumber against the fence so the wood glides smoothly and is flush against it at all points as you push it forward. Never allow your fingers to come within 6 inches of the blade; use a push stick when you come to the end of the cut (see page 124).

2 MAKE A CROSSCUT.

Make sure the miter gauge is exactly perpendicular to the blade; slip it into its channel and square it using the edge of the table as a guide. Set the blade depth ¼ inch above the board and start the motor. Hold the board firmly against the miter guide and slide the wood toward the blade. Hold the board only at the miter gauge. If you hold the wood on both sides of the cut, the blade may bind, causing dangerous kickback. Keep your fingers well away from the blade.

TABLESAW, RADIAL-ARM SAW, OR POWER MITERSAW?

A tablesaw and a power mitersaw make an ideal combination. With a tablesaw, you can make long straight cuts with ease. A tablesaw also is superior for cutting dadoes. With a power mitersaw, you can crosscut long narrow pieces easily—a task that can be difficult with a tablesaw.

A radial-arm saw does the jobs of a tablesaw and power mitersaw, but not quite as well. It crosscuts with less precision than a mitersaw. Cutting angles other than 90 degrees may be a problem. Making long rip cuts in sheets of plywood also is difficult.

CAUTION

SAFETY MEASURES FOR A TABLESAW

Because a tablesaw runs so smoothly and seems so stable, it's easy to let safety consciousness lapse while working with one. A tablesaw is a tool worthy of respect; careless use can injure anyone, whether a beginner or an experienced user.

Always keep your fingers well away from the blade. Never wear long sleeves or loose clothing while using a tablesaw. Never reach across the saw blade while it is running. Keep push sticks and an anti-kickback featherboard handy and develop the habit of using them (see page 124). Turn off the saw and let the blade stop when you need to free a piece of wood that has become stuck.

Using a tablesaw *(continued)*

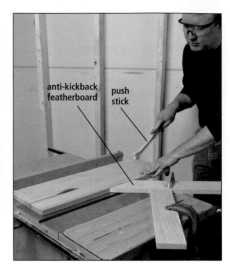

anti-kickback featherboard   push stick

MAKE A BEVELED RIP CUT.

To set the bevel, use an adjustable bevel gauge or mark the bevel angle on the end of the board and tilt the blade until it aligns with the mark. Hold the board against the blade at the correct location, slide the fence against the board, and lock the fence in place. Follow the same procedures as for a rip cut (see page 123).

ADJUST THE BLADE DEPTH.

Before every cut, adjust the blade depth so it is about ¼ inch above the top of the board you are cutting. This makes a cleaner cut and helps avoid binding and dangerous kickback. If you are cutting a sheet of plywood that is warped, you may need to raise the blade higher so it cuts through the sheet completely at all points. Always unplug the tablesaw before making blade adjustments.

USE PUSH STICKS AND A FEATHERBOARD.

To make a featherboard, cut one end of a 16-inch-long 1×6 at 60 degrees, then cut 8-inch-long kerfs ¼ inch apart into the angled end. When clamped as shown *above*, it ensures a straight cut and prevents kickback in case the blade binds. Make push sticks out of 1× lumber or ½-inch plywood or buy commercial ones and use them to keep your hands well clear of the blade.

CUT DADOES, RABBETS, AND TENONS.

With a dado blade, you can make a variety of groove sizes. With a regular dado blade, sandwich a combination of chippers between the two outside cutter blades to get your desired width. To set the blade to the desired depth, mark the depth on the board and hold it next to the blade as you adjust it. Adjustable dado blades dial to the desired width.

If you need to make a groove wider than the dado blade, make repeated passes, moving the board a little less than the width of the blade for each pass.

On a tablesaw, you will not be able to see the cut as you make it, so test your settings on a scrap piece to make sure the dado is the correct width and depth. Then make the real cut.

Dado or groove

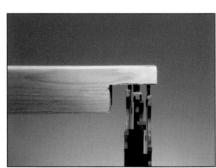

Rabbet

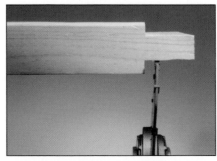

Tenon made with an adjustable dado blade

USING A RADIAL-ARM SAW

A radial-arm saw works best for crosscutting wood, but you can use it for ripping as well, as long as you take it slowly and use precautions (see *below right*). With attachments available on some models, you can use a radial-arm saw as a router or a sander.

A radial-arm saw table is made of particleboard or plywood rather than metal because the saw blade must cut into the table slightly to cut boards completely. When the tabletop becomes shredded after years of use, you should replace it. The fence, usually a piece of 1×2, needs to be replaced more often.

A power mitersaw can make some of the same cuts as a radial-arm saw, but it is designed for two purposes only: miter-cutting and crosscutting small-width boards (usually 1×6 or smaller). A power mitersaw is more portable than a radial-arm saw and sets up easily on a couple of sawhorses for cutting moldings at the site.

MAKE A MITER CUT OR CROSSCUT.

Test your saw for accuracy by cutting scraps at 45 and 90 degrees and adjust the fence or the saw if necessary. To make the cut, hold the board firmly against the fence. Make sure the board is fully supported and lies flat on the table. Pull the saw toward you, cutting the board so the saw kerf is on the scrap side of the line.

CUT A DADO OR RABBET.

To cut a notch for a dado or rabbet, raise the blade to the desired height; test the cut depth on a scrap. Check that the board lies flat; any warp will distort the cut. Cut on each side of the notch, then make a series of cuts in the interior. Clean out the notch with a chisel. If you have many notches to cut, use dado blades.

MAKE A RIP CUT OR BEVELED RIP CUT.

Turn the saw so the blade rotates up against the board, the opposite of a crosscut or dado cut. Start the saw with the blade slightly raised above the tabletop, then lower it to the cut line. To avoid kickback, hold the board firmly as you feed it into the blade. Pull the board through the blade to finish the cut.

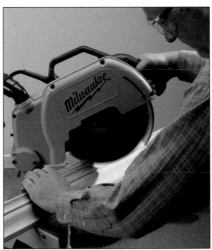

CUT MOLDING WITH A POWER MITERSAW.

A power mitersaw is convenient for cutting molding. Hold the piece firmly against the fence, start the saw, and lower the blade to make the cut. (See page 117.) The cut will often begin at the middle of a molding; make your marks accordingly. Hold crown molding, at the correct angle for cutting with triangular blocks.

▼ CAUTION

RADIAL-ARM SAW SAFETY

Radial-arm and power mitersaws can be extremely dangerous. Not only can you cut yourself with the blades, but a radial-arm saw almost certainly will kick a board back at bulletlike speed if you are not careful. Develop these safety habits:

- Never remove the saw guard. Take the time to adjust the guard for maximum safety before making each cut.
- When ripping boards with a radial-arm saw, use a push stick and featherboard like those for a tablesaw (see page 124). Also stand to the side of the board so if it shoots back, it won't hit you.
- Keep work well supported so the blade will not bind.

USING A ROUTER

With the versatility and power of a router, you can custom-design and mill lumber to your own specifications. In addition to choosing from a number of bits (shown *below*), you can set your bit to the depth of cut that suits you. Often, it's possible to save money by milling your own lumber rather than buying expensive moldings. For rounding off edges, a router produces a far more professional-looking finish than does a rasp or sander.

CAUTION

BITS ARE SHARP!

Most of the time, you will not even see your router bit as you work. Don't let that lull you into complacency: A router's sharp bit, rotating at tremendous speed, can do major damage in a millisecond. Keep your hands well away from the work.

USE A GUIDE.

You can make accurate cuts using a router guide. Sometimes a simple straightedge will suffice; just hold the baseplate tight against it as you cut. A guide like the one shown allows you to follow a precut template. You may want to purchase a router table, which holds the router in an upside-down position; you can adjust and operate it much as you would a tablesaw.

USE SPECIALTY GUIDES.

Numerous guides are available for special purposes. To cut smooth circles or curves, use a trammel-point guide like the one shown. A router bit spins clockwise, so you will get the best results if you move the router counterclockwise. You also can buy guides for cutting dovetail joints or hinge mortises.

Chamfer

Core box

Corner round

Dado

Dovetail

Flush trim

Plunge cut

Rabbet

Straight bit

V-groove

CHOOSING A ROUTER

As a general rule, the more power a router has, the cleaner and faster it will cut. A variable-speed router has some advantages because some bits are designed to be used at lower speeds than others.

Buy a model that can be attached to a table easily or that has a variety of guides you can assemble quickly. Why spend half your work time setting up the router?

Be sure you can change bits and adjust the router depth easily.

CHOOSE AMONG MANY BITS.

Piloted bits, such as the flush trim, rabbet, chamfer, and corner round, are self-guiding; you don't need to use a guide or template when cutting with them. Use these bits to shape edges of boards or to cut laminates after they have been applied. Bits with ball-bearing guides usually work more smoothly.

The other bits shown require a guide or template. You can use two or more bits in succession to make intricate shapes.

DRILLING

Some carpenters still haul out a brace and auger bit to bore a hole, but for most the electric drill is the tool of choice. With a variable-speed power drill, you can drill a hole of about any size, drive screws into wood or metal, buff and grind, and even mix paint or mortar.

Some carpenters keep two drills on hand—one for drilling pilot holes, the other for driving screws. That way they don't waste time changing bits. A power drill with a keyless chuck speeds up a bit change, although you may find bits slip during heavy-duty tasks.

For perfectly perpendicular holes, you'll need a drill press. But if you learn the techniques here and on the next three pages, you can bore holes that are straight enough for household carpentry.

CHOOSING A DRILL

- Avoid buying a low-quality drill with a ¼-inch chuck. It will not have the power you need and will soon burn out. One tip-off to a better quality tool is the cord. Look for a long cord that flexes more like rubber than plastic.
- A hammer drill, or a drill with a hammer option, bangs at the material as it drills. It's useful when drilling in masonry.
- A cordless drill can make your work easier, but only if it is powerful enough to do most things that a corded drill can do.
- Specialized tasks often require a high-speed drill (one with high revolutions per minute). For

example, self-tapping steel stud screws (see page 68) require a drill that runs at least 2,500 rpm.
- For heavy-duty work, choose a corded drill with a ½-inch chuck. This will run at a lower speed but will have more power than a standard 3⁄8-inch drill.
- For additional information on choosing a drill, see page 85.
- Some tools that look like drills are actually screwdrivers. The most common are designed for driving drywall screws. These set the head of the screw at the required depth—deep enough to make an indentation but not so deep that it damages the drywall.

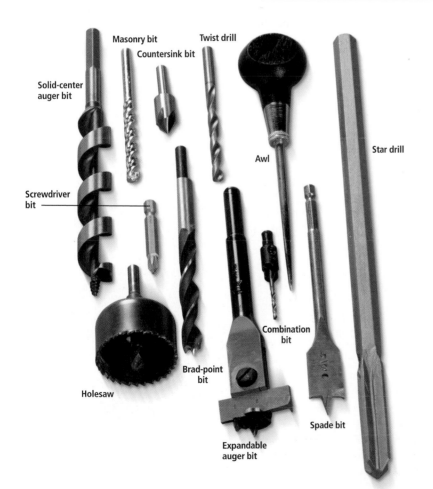

Solid-center auger bit

Masonry bit

Countersink bit

Twist drill

Awl

Star drill

Screwdriver bit

Combination bit

Holesaw

Brad-point bit

Spade bit

Expandable auger bit

CHOOSE THE CORRECT BIT.

Shown at *left* are some of the more common drill bits. **Auger bits,** either solid-center or **expandable,** are designed to be used with a hand brace, as is a **screwdriver bit.** For holes ½ inch or smaller in diameter, use **twist drills.** A **brad-point bit** makes a cleaner hole in wood than a twist drill. For holes from ½ to 1¼ inches in diameter, use a **spade bit.** For making holes in masonry or concrete, use a carbide-tipped **masonry bit** or a **star drill,** which you drive with a hammer. A **countersink bit** bores a shallow hole so you can set screw heads flush with or below the surface. A **combination bit** drills both a pilot hole and a countersink hole in one step. Use a simple **awl** to prepare the way for a small screw. For holes larger than 1¼ inches and/or for drilling precise holes through tough materials, use a **holesaw.**

Drilling (continued)

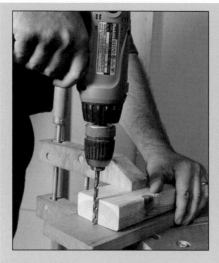

MAKE A STARTER HOLE.

Drill bits tend to skate away when you begin boring holes, so make a shallow starter hole with an awl or a center punch. In softwoods, a gentle tap on an awl with the palm of your hand will do the job. On hardwoods or metal, you may need to tap the center punch or awl with a hammer.

IMPROVISE A GUIDE.

Usually you'll want to drill holes perpendicular to the board. Check the bit for square as it enters the material by clamping a piece of square-cut scrap lumber in place, as shown. With some drills, you can hold a square on the material and against the body of the drill. When you need to drill a hole at an angle, fashion a guide by cutting the edge of a piece of scrap lumber to the desired angle. Clamp the guide so it aligns the tip of the bit exactly on your center mark. Begin the hole by drilling perpendicular to the surface. Once you have gone deep enough to keep the bit from skating away, shift the drill to the angle.

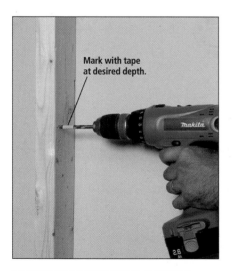

Mark with tape at desired depth.

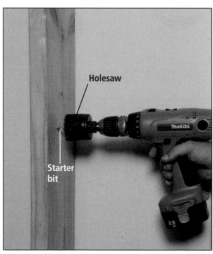

Holesaw

Starter bit

MARK THE BIT FOR DEPTH.

When you want to drill one or more holes to a certain depth, wrap masking or electrical tape around your drill bit so the bottom edge of the tape contacts the surface of the material when the bit is at the desired depth. Drill with gentle pressure. Back the bit out as soon as the tape touches the surface of the material.

USE A HOLESAW.

When drilling large-diameter holes with a holesaw, make a starter hole on your center mark to guide the starter bit. To ensure that the other side of the material doesn't splinter when the bit penetrates it, clamp a piece of scrap stock against the other side. Or drill until the pilot bit pokes through, then drill from the other side.

CAUTION

AVOID DAMAGING YOUR DRILL BITS AND DRILL

Drilling is a simple procedure, but it's easy to dull or break a drill bit. Be careful not to overheat the bit; an overheated bit will become dull quickly. If you see smoke, stop drilling immediately. Pause once in a while and test the bit for heat by quickly tapping it with your finger.

Unlike a professional model, a homeowner-type drill is not designed for constant use. If you feel the body of the drill heating up, stop and give it a rest or you could burn it out.

Hold the drill firmly upright as you work. If you tip the tool while drilling, there's a good chance the bit will break.

Drill until point of spade bit barely pierces material.

Drill from the other side to complete the hole.

Back up to pull wood particles out.

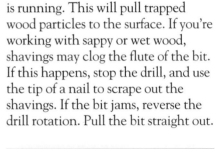

Clean particles from the flute.

AVOID SPLINTERS WITH A SPADE BIT.

When using a spade bit, drill through the material until the tip of the bit begins to poke out the backside of the material. Carefully reverse the bit out of the hole. Complete the hole by drilling from the other side, using the pilot hole you've just made.

KEEP PARTICLES FROM CLOGGING HOLE.

When you drill deep holes into thick material, wood particles build up in the hole, clogging the bit and causing it to bind. Don't force the bit in farther than it wants to go or you will burn it out. Instead feed the bit into the wood slowly and back out of the hole frequently while the drill motor is running. This will pull trapped wood particles to the surface. If you're working with sappy or wet wood, shavings may clog the flute of the bit. If this happens, stop the drill, and use the tip of a nail to scrape out the shavings. If the bit jams, reverse the drill rotation. Pull the bit straight out.

1. Drill pilot hole.

2. Enlarge for screw.

3. Countersink for screw head.

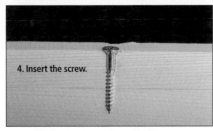

4. Insert the screw.

For flush screw heads, drill to this point.

For countersunk screw heads, drill to this point.

FOR THE BEST FIT, DRILL THREE HOLES...

When you use wood screws to fasten two pieces of material together, take the time to provide clearance for the screw to ensure easy driving and to avoid splits. Using a bit that is slightly smaller than the screw, drill through the top and bottom piece. Then select a bit that is as thick as the screw shank and drill through the top board. The screw should slide easily through this top hole and grip tightly as it passes into the smaller hole. Use a countersink bit to bore a space for the screw head. When you drive the screw, it will fit without cracking the wood.

OR USE A COMBINATION BIT.

If you're driving a number of screws, buy a combination countersink-counterbore bit, which drills three holes in one action. Be sure to get the correct bits for the screws you will be driving. If you want the screw head to be flush with the surface, drill until the spot marked on the bit, *above*, is even with the surface. To counterbore the screw head, drill deeper.

Drilling *(continued)*

DRILL INTO MASONRY AND CONCRETE.

Use a masonry bit when drilling into brick or concrete surfaces. Usually, brick is easy to drill into and concrete is more difficult. Check the bit often to make sure it's not overheating. If you see smoke, stop immediately.

Here is a trick that works surprisingly well: Spray the bit and the hole with window cleaner as you work. This keeps the bit cool, and the foaming action of the cleaner brings debris up and out of the hole.

Occasionally when drilling into concrete, you will run into an especially hard spot (usually a rock embedded in the concrete). Take the bit out, insert a masonry nail or thin cold chisel, and bang with a hammer to crack the rock and give your bit a place to grab. If you have much masonry drilling to do, buy a hammer drill, which bangs as you drill.

DRILL THROUGH CERAMIC TILE.

Wall tiles are usually soft, but floor tiles can be tough. Nick the surface of the tile just enough so the bit will not wander as you drill. Keep the bit and the hole lubricated with a few drops of oil. Use a masonry bit or a special tile bit like the one shown *above*.

Bit with lead screw

Expandable bit for brace

USE A BRACE AND EXPANDABLE BIT.

A brace is an old-fashioned tool that works faster than you may expect. To drill large-diameter holes, bore until the lead screw of the bit pokes through the material. Then drill through from the other side. To get more pressure on the brace, hold its head against your body and lean into the work.

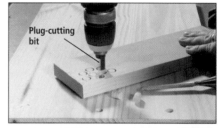

Plug-cutting bit

BORE AND PLUG FOR A FINISHED LOOK.

For a handcrafted appearance, drill pilot holes, then drill a wooden plug using a plug-cutting bit. Drive the screw in, squirt a little white glue into the hole, and tap in the plug. Allow the plug to stick out slightly. After the glue has dried, chisel and sand the plug flush with the surface.

NAILING

The quickest way to make a job look shoddy and amateurish is to make a nailing mistake that mars the wood. All your careful measuring and cutting will be for naught if the wood ends up with "smiles" and "frowns" made by a hammer that missed the nail or if you bend a nail while driving it.

Professional carpenters make nailing look easy—and for good reason. When properly done, pounding a nail home is not a struggle but is done with smooth, fluid motions. You may never be as fast at nailing as professionals because they get plenty of practice, but you can learn to drive nails without damaging the material or yourself.

SET THE NAIL.

Practice on scrap pieces before you pound nails into finished work. To ensure that the hammer strikes the nail and not your fingers and that the nail will be driven into the board squarely, hold the nail vertically and grip the hammer near the end of the handle. Lightly tap the nail until it stands by itself.

If you must drive a nail near the end of a board, reduce the risk of splitting the wood by drilling a pilot hole or blunting the nail point. (Turn the nail upside down and tap the point with the hammer.)

PROPER TECHNIQUE MAKES NAILING EASY.

Once the nail is set in place, remove your hand from it. Keep your eye on the nail as you swing the hammer, letting the weight of the hammerhead do the driving.

Beginners tend to hold a hammer stiffly and keep their shoulders rigid, swinging from the elbow. This leads to a tired, sore arm and to mistakes. Loosen up. Your whole arm should move as you swing from the shoulder. Keep your wrist loose so you can give the hammer a final snap at the end of each blow. The entire motion should be relaxed and smooth.

With the last hammer blow, push the head of the nail flush or nearly flush with the surface of the wood. The convex shape of the hammer face allows you to do this without marring the surface.

GETTING THE HOLDING POWER YOU NEED

How well a nail holds in wood depends on how much of its surface contacts the wood. The longer and thicker the nail, the better it will hold.

When possible, use the Rule of Three: A nail should be three times as long as the thickness of the board being fastened. Two-thirds of the nail then will be in the board to which you are fastening the first one. If the nail must penetrate through empty space or drywall, increase the nail length by that distance.

A thick nail holds better but not if it splits the wood. In that case, most of its holding power is lost. Special nails, such as ringshank and cement-coated nails, hold better than standard nails. A headed nail holds better than a finishing nail, which has no head.

Nailing *(continued)*

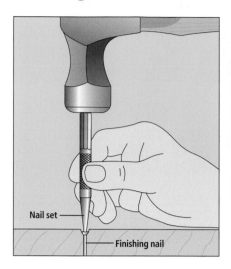

COUNTERSINK FINISHING NAILS.

In most cases, it's best to drive the heads of finishing or casing nails below the surface. You can fill the holes with wood putty later. This takes little time and leads to a much better looking finish than nails driven flush. Hold a nail set against the nailhead and tap it in.

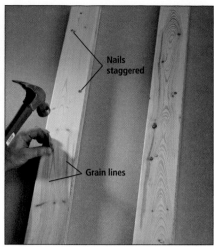

STAGGER NAILS TO AVOID SPLITS.

When driving several nails along the length of a board, stagger them so you don't split the board. The idea is to avoid pounding neighboring nails through the same grain line; two nails will stress the grain twice as much as one nail. If the work will be visible, stagger the nails in a pattern.

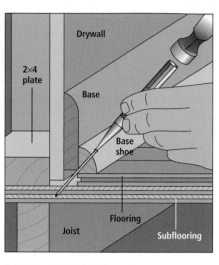

DRILL PILOT HOLES.

When you nail within 2 inches of the end of a board or into hardwood, drill pilot holes to avoid splitting the wood. Pilot holes should be slightly smaller than the diameter of the nail. When attaching a base shoe, drive nails into pilot holes so they miss the flooring, which needs room to expand and contract with changes in temperature and humidity.

USING MASONRY NAILS

Masonry nails attach materials to concrete, brick, and masonry block. With flat masonry nails, be sure to turn the nail in the direction of the grain so it's less likely to split the wood.

You can use a standard hammer, but the job is easier with a heavy mallet. Hold the board in place and drive the masonry nail through it. Once the nail hits the masonry surface, strike it with hard strokes. With subsequent nails, check to see whether you have dislodged any nails; you may have to drive more.

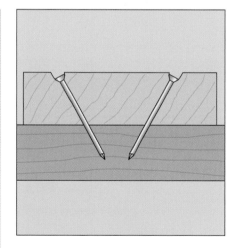

SKEW NAILS FOR A STRONGER HOLD.

In situations where you cannot use as long a nail as you would like, drive nails at an angle. Drive one nail at about a 60-degree angle in one direction, then drive in another one in the opposite direction. The skewed nails will work together, making it difficult to pull the board loose. Set the nailheads into the surface for a finished appearance.

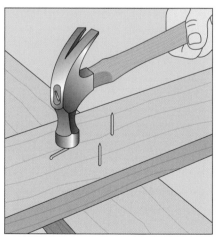

CLINCH NAILS FOR THE BEST HOLD.

If looks are not important but strength is, use nails about 1 inch longer than the thickness of the pieces you're fastening. Drive the nails, then turn the boards over and bend the exposed portion of the nails so they are nearly flush with the surface and parallel to the wood grain. The resulting joint will be extremely difficult to pull apart.

FASTENING WITH SCREWS

It's easy to see why screws fasten so well: The threads grip wood fibers in a way that a smooth nail cannot. When a screw is driven home, the threads exert tremendous pressure against the screw head to hold the fastener firmly in place. With the right tools (see box, *below*), driving screws can be almost as quick as nailing. If you make a mistake, it's easy to remove a screw without damaging your work. Screws must be driven with care, however. If you do not start out straight, there is no way to correct the mistake as you continue driving the screw. Without a pilot hole, the screw may split the wood and the screw will not hold securely. If the pilot hole is too large, the screw will not grip well.

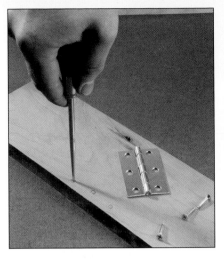

MAKE A STARTER HOLE WITH AN AWL.

Small screws seldom require pilot holes (see the box, *below right*). But, they do need a starter hole. Poke a hole with a scratch awl. Give it a few twists, back it out, and you're ready to drive the screw. Drill a pilot hole in hardwood, such as oak or maple.

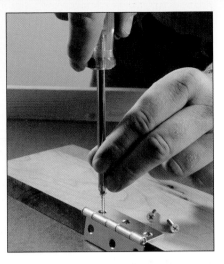

HOLD THE SCREWDRIVER INSTEAD OF THE SCREW.

Start screws by holding the screwdriver handle with one hand and the screwdriver blade with the other. Don't hold the screw. If the screw is spinning around and not going into the wood, put two hands on the handle to apply more pressure.

POWER-DRIVING MAKES ASSEMBLY GO FASTER.

Even a few screws can take a long time to drive by hand, so consider using a drill with a screwdriver bit. When driving slotted screws, take care that the bit does not wander partway out of the slot, or you could damage the surface into which you are screwing. Take your time, or the bit may slip out of the slot. Maintain firm, even pressure as you work.

TOOLS TO USE

Power-driven screws hold tightly, go in quickly, and are easy to remove. Here are some tools that make working with them even more convenient:

- A variable-speed, reversible drill starts the screws slowly and removes them if necessary.

- With a magnetic sleeve, screws stick to the bit, making it easy to drive them in hard-to-reach places. Changing bit tips is easy: Simply press them into the sleeve.

- Have on hand a collection of drill bits, particularly No. 1 and No. 2 phillips bits as well as some slotted bits.

- Consider buying square-head screws and bits. These bits fit into and grab the screw slot better than phillips-head and slotted screws.

WHEN DO YOU NEED A PILOT HOLE?

If there is a danger of cracking the wood, you should always drill a pilot hole, no matter how small the screw. For instance, if the wood is brittle or if you will be driving a screw near the end of a board, almost any screw can split the wood. But if you are drilling into a sound board at a spot 2 inches or more from its end, it usually will be safe to drive in a No. 6 or thinner screw without a pilot hole. If you are drilling into plywood or framing lumber, you should be able to drive No. 8 screws without pilot holes. You should always drill a pilot hole in hardwood to prevent breaking the screw For advice on selecting the correct-size bit, see page 101.

Fastening with screws *(continued)*

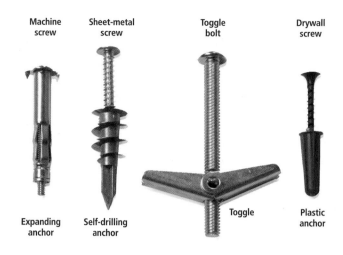

Machine screw · Sheet-metal screw · Toggle bolt · Drywall screw

Expanding anchor · Self-drilling anchor · Toggle · Plastic anchor

USE PHILLIPS-HEAD DRYWALL SCREWS.

You can buy drywall screws by the pound at bargain prices and use them in most places you would use nails. If you use a magnetic sleeve, place the screw on the bit first, then set the tip of the screw in place on the material. If you need to hold the screw, hold the head only, not the sharp threads. Particleboard screws are handy too; they countersink themselves.

ATTACH ITEMS TO WALLS WITH SPECIAL FASTENERS.

If you need to attach something to a wall, the ideal way is to drive a screw into a stud. But often that's not possible. The screws and bolts shown *above* are designed to hold items firmly in drywall or plaster walls. To use expanding anchors and plastic anchors, drill holes and tap the unit into the wall; the anchor will spread and grip as you tighten the screw.

Use self-drilling anchors only in drywall. You don't need to drill a hole; just screw the anchor in and insert a screw. To use a toggle bolt, drill a hole large enough for the folded-back toggles to fit through. Push the toggles through the hole and turn the bolt until the toggles snug up to the backside of the wall.

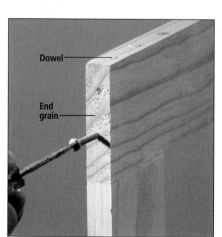

Dowel

End grain

SCREW INTO END GRAIN.

When a fastener is driven into the end grain of a board, it will not hold as well as it does across the grain because it runs parallel to the grain rather than at an angle to it. Use a longer screw than you usually would. Where holding power is critical, drill a hole and install a dowel, as shown, into which you can drive the screw.

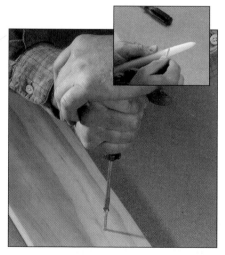

BEAR DOWN ON HARD-TO-DRIVE SCREWS.

If the going gets tough, the screw may stop turning. Exert pressure on the screwdriver with the palm of one hand and turn it with the other. If you still can't drive the screw, remove it and drill a slightly larger pilot hole. Another solution is to lubricate the threads with candle wax and try again.

FASTENING TO METAL WITH SCREWS

For fastening thin sheet metal or soft metal, such as brass, use sheet-metal screws (see page 68). Drill a hole of the correct size through the pieces (see page 130) and drive in the screw. Some screws are self-drilling; you simply drive the screw and it drills through the metal.

For heavier metals, drill a pilot hole through the metal then drive in a self-tapping screw.

For metal ⅛ inch or thicker and where you want a strong joint, buy a tap and a drill bit of the correct size. The tap cuts machine-screw threads into a hole so you can screw in a machine screw or bolt.

FASTENING WITH BOLTS

Nails and screws depend on friction between the fastener and the wood to do their job. When you tighten a nut on a bolt, however, you're actually clamping adjoining members together, producing the sturdiest of all joints. All types of bolts require a hole bored through both pieces being joined together. This page provides information about installing machine and carriage bolts. For help with toggle bolts and other anchors, see page 134.

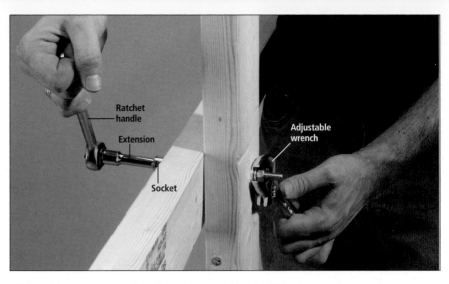

CAUTION

DON'T OVERTIGHTEN.

Overtightening bolts can strip threads and damage wood, reducing the holding power of the bolt. Tighten the nut and bolt firmly against the wood, give them another half-turn, then stop.

FASTEN PARTS TOGETHER WITH MACHINE BOLTS.

Machine bolts have hexagonal heads and threads running partway or all the way along the shank. When fastening wood together, slip a flat washer onto the bolt and slide the bolt through the holes in the parts. Add another flat washer, then a lock washer. Screw the nut on and tighten it. The flat washers keep the nut and the bolt head from biting into the wood. The lock washer prevents the nut from coming loose. Use two wrenches to draw the nut onto the bolt: one to steady the nut, the other to turn the bolt head.

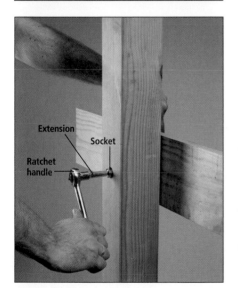

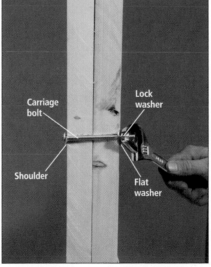

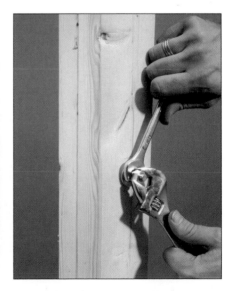

TIGHTEN A COUNTERSUNK BOLT HEAD.

To install a machine bolt in a hard-to-get-at place or when you countersink the bolt head, use a socket wrench with a socket extension to reach into the recess. Hold the nut with another wrench.

INSTALL A CARRIAGE BOLT.

A carriage bolt has a plain, round head with a square shank below it. Insert it into the hole and tap the head flush with the surface. Slip a flat washer, a lock washer, and a nut onto the bolt. Tighten the nut. The square shoulder keeps the bolt from spinning as the nut is tightened. No washer is needed under the head. The lock washer should keep the nut from working loose. As added protection, thread another nut onto the bolt, snug it against the first, then jam the nuts by turning them in opposite directions, as shown above.

REMOVING NAILS AND SCREWS

Mistakes are a part of every carpenter's day. In fact, knowing how to undo mistakes is one of the hallmarks of an experienced carpenter, and that necessitates a good knowledge of how to remove nails and screws. Whether you're correcting mistakes, disassembling an old structure, or recycling used lumber, you'll find it's worth it to learn how to remove fasteners quickly and neatly.

Removing screws often is just a matter of reversing your drill and screwing the old fastener out. However, you may be faced with a stripped head or an extra-tight screw (see page 137).

Most commonly, you'll be faced with removing nails. Don't just start whacking away in frustration, or you'll damage the wood. Use these methods and accept that nail removal is a normal part of a carpenter's job.

PRY WITH A FLAT BAR.

If the head of the nail has not been set into the wood, it may be possible to shoehorn a flat bar under it and pry up the nail. Tap the notch of the chisel-like head of the bar under the nailhead and pull back on the bar. Because of its smooth, flat body, a pry bar makes only a slight indentation in the board as you remove the nail.

USE A WOOD BLOCK.

There are two good reasons for using a wood block when removing a nail. First, the raised height gives your hammer extra leverage, making it much easier to pull the nail out. Second, the block protects your work. Without it, the head of the hammer would dig in and make an unsightly indentation.

Pound so claws grab nailhead.

DIG NAILS OUT WITH A CAT'S PAW.

A cat's paw removes nails that are embedded deeply in lumber. Its drawback is that it must bite deeply into the wood to grip the nailhead. Place the clawed tip behind the nailhead at a 45-degree angle. Pound the claws under the nailhead, pry the nail partway out, then use a hammer and block.

Tap out to release nails.

Tap in to expose nailheads.

POUND OUT BOARD TO LOOSEN NAILS.

If you can reach the backside of the joined material, strike the joint from behind, then hammer the members back together from the front. This usually pops the nailheads out far enough for you to grip them with your hammer claw.

Tight-work hacksaw

CUT NAILS.

Where access is tight, sometimes you can disjoin two members by sawing through the nails. If you have a reciprocating saw with a metal-cutting blade, this will be easy. Otherwise use a tight-work hacksaw. After you break the joint, use a nail set to force the heads out, then remove the nails.

Nail set

Putty knife

PUNCH THROUGH AND PRY.

To avoid splitting molding, punch the finishing nails that hold it in place through it with a nail set or pin punch. Try not to make the hole larger; use a small-diameter nail set. Pound the head of the finishing nail deeply into the molding. You'll feel the board come loose. Once you have punched the nails through, pry off the molding with a putty knife or chisel, taking care not to mar the wood.

CLEAN OUT A PAINTED SCREW HEAD.

When removing old screws that have been painted, take the time to clean the paint out of the slots. If you don't clean the head, you may strip the screw head, making it even more difficult to remove. Place a screwdriver as shown *above* and tap with a hammer.

REMOVING OLD SCREWS

Here are some tips for removing stubborn screws:

For a slotted screw that has been stripped so much that a screwdriver can't get a good hold, deepen the slot by cutting into it with a hacksaw.

Extremely tight screws often can be loosened with heat. Hold the tip of a soldering gun against the screw head for a minute or two, then try loosening it.

For stripped phillips-head screws, it sometimes helps to drill a small hole in the center of the head to give the screwdriver more to grip.

For an extremely stubborn screw, buy a screw and bolt extracting tool. Drill a small hole in the screw head, insert the tool, turn it with a wrench, and twist the screw out.

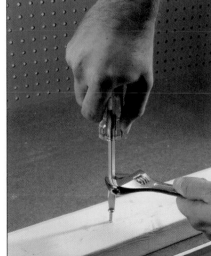

ADD FORCE TO A SCREWDRIVER.

If you need greater turning power, use a screwdriver with a square shank and an adjustable wrench. Adjust the wrench so it fits tightly on the screwdriver. Press down on the handle of the screwdriver with the palm of your hand as you turn with the wrench.

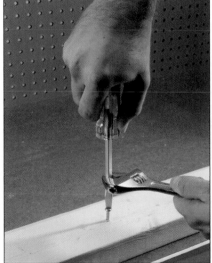

CUT A STUBBORN NUT.

Rusty or damaged bolt threads make it hard to remove a nut. You can solve the problem quickly with a hacksaw. Align the saw blade so it rubs against the threads and cut down through the nut. You will cut off about one-third of the nut. Once you have done this, it will be easy to knock the nut loose or unscrew it.

GLUING AND CLAMPING

A joint will be stronger if you use glue in addition to nails or screws. For some projects, glue alone will be enough.

Read the label before you purchase a bottle of glue. You want the project to be successful, and so does the glue manufacturer. Printed on the label you will find detailed information about each type of glue. The label will state if the glue is appropriate for your project. It also will tell you what safety precautions to take when using the glue.

Use contact cement to attach wood veneers or plastic laminates to wood surfaces. Apply the cement to both surfaces and let them dry. Align the parts precisely before you join them—the first bond is permanent (see pages 147–148). Use paneling adhesives to attach sheet goods to walls (see pages 78–79). For interior projects, use carpenter's glue with aliphatic resin. This is superior to standard white glue because it sets up faster, resists heat and moisture better, and is stronger. For the glue to work, however, the pieces must be clamped together firmly until the glue sets.

For those times when you wish you had a third hand to hold a workpiece, using a clamp is the answer. A clamp helps grip objects while you work on them. It also will hold a project tightly together while glue sets. The amount of time a clamp has to remain in place depends on the type of adhesive, room temperature and humidity, and the complexity of the project. Follow the glue manufacturer's suggestion for clamping. If the manufacturer says to clamp 24 hours, give the glue 24 hours to set. The result of shorting the time may be disastrous.

(see pages 147–148)
(see pages 78–79)

CLAMPING TIPS

Dry-fit pieces to make sure they align correctly before gluing and clamping.

Use as many clamps as you need to make sure that the glued surfaces remain squeezed together tightly at all points. Wipe off excess glue with a damp rag.

Apply just enough clamping pressure to create a tight bond; don't distort the wood.

Recheck the fit after tightening the clamps, then make any necessary adjustments.

CHECK THE EXPIRATION DATE

Glue failure rarely happens, but when it does, one of two things has occurred: Either you used the wrong glue for the job, or it has exceeded its shelf life. The shelf life of glue varies. The standard shelf life is one year. Some have a shelf life as short as three months. If you have forgotten when you bought the bottle of glue, dispose of it properly and buy a new bottle. Mark the date on it, thus taking the guesswork out of later trying to remember when you bought it.

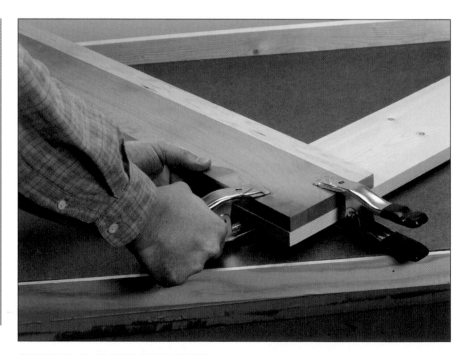

SPRING CLAMPS GRIP FAST.

For light work, these are the easiest clamps to use. Apply glue to both pieces and place them together in correct alignment. Squeeze the clamp handles to spread the jaws. When you release the handles, the springs will clamp the work together. You may want to have several sizes of these inexpensive clamps on hand.

HAND-SCREW CLAMPS ADJUST TO FIT ANGLED PIECES.

These clamps work well for cabinetmaking and other woodworking projects. Because their jaws are made of wood, you need not worry about marring your project—as long as the jaw faces are clean. Adjust a clamp to almost any size or angle simply by turning its two hand screws.

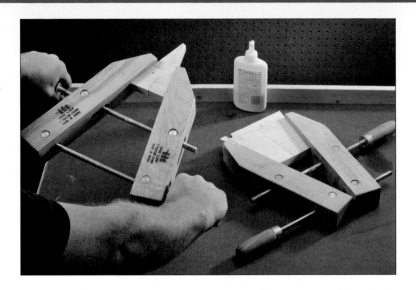

USE THE RIGHT CLAMP FOR THE JOB.

C-clamps are inexpensive and work well when the pieces are not too wide. Use blocks of wood to keep the clamps from marring the boards. For miter joints, use **miter clamps** that hold the boards at a 90-degree angle.

For large projects, use **pipe clamps.** You should alternate them as shown to prevent buckling. A **strap clamp** works well for cabinetry projects. It will clamp several joints at once without marring the wood.

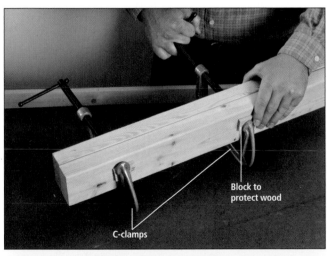

Block to protect wood

C-clamps

Pipe clamps

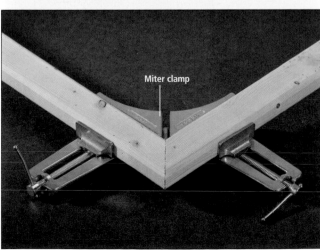

Miter clamp

Strap clamp

CAULKING AND APPLYING ADHESIVE

It takes practice to lay down a clean-looking bead of caulk. Practice on scrap materials or start in an inconspicuous area before you caulk an area that is highly visible.

Choose among numerous adhesives that are designed for particular jobs (see the chart, *below left*). When working with adhesives, be careful to apply them smoothly and evenly so the piece will adhere uniformly. Avoid applying too much adhesive; cleaning up messes can take longer than the initial job.

YOU'LL NEED

TIME: About 20 minutes to caulk around a bathtub or countertop, 10 to 30 minutes to adhere laminate or paneling.

SKILLS: Smooth, steady control.

TOOLS: Utility knife, caulking gun, notched trowel.

APPLY A BEAD OF CAULK.

Make sure the joint to be caulked is free of dirt and grease and no gaps wider than your bead of caulk are present. Snip the nozzle of the caulk tube at about a 45-degree angle. The closer to the tip you cut, the smaller the bead will be. You may need to puncture the inside seal with a long nail. Squeeze the caulking gun handle until caulk starts coming out; move smoothly to apply an even bead.

ATTACH PANELING TO WALLS WITH ADHESIVE.

To attach paneling to walls, apply a bead of adhesive on either the wall or the back of the panel. Use a notched trowel or make a squiggle pattern using a caulking gun. Press the panel against the wall, then pull it out slightly. Wait a few minutes for the adhesive to get tacky (the manufacturer's instructions will tell you how long), then press the panel against the wall again.

COVER LARGE AREAS WITH A NOTCHED TROWEL.

For a smooth, even application, use a notched trowel to apply adhesives. Check the adhesive container for the type and size of notches the trowel should have. Hold the trowel nearly parallel to the surface to make sure the adhesive sticks. Tilt the trowel up at about a 45-degree angle and press firmly to spread the adhesive.

SELECTING ADHESIVES

Adhesive Type	Primary Use	Holding Power	Moisture Resistance	Set/Cure Time	Type of Applicator
Contact cement	Applying wood veneer and plastic laminate.	Excellent	Excellent	Must dry first / 1–2 days	Brush, notched trowel, or paint roller
Epoxy adhesive	Bonding almost any materials. Must mix the parts.	Excellent	Good	30 minutes / 1–10 hours	Throwaway brush or flat stick
Panel adhesive	Attaching drywall or paneling to walls.	Good	Fair	1 hour / 24 hours	Caulk tube or notched trowel
Carpenter's glue	Bonding wood together for small projects.	Good	Fair	30 minutes / 24 hours	Squeeze-type container
Cyanoacrylate (superglue)	Bonding small items of almost any material.	Good	Fair	1–2 minutes / 24 hours	Squeeze tube

MAKING SIMPLE, STRONG JOINTS

Strong, good-looking wood joints are essential to all carpentry and woodworking projects. Here are some of the simplest and strongest joinery methods. Each of these joints can be made with hand tools, but if you have shop tools, such as a tablesaw or power mitersaw, the job will go faster and the joint will be tighter. None requires cabinetmaking expertise.

You'll need to hone your measuring, cutting, and fastening skills to make neat, sturdy joints. See pages 106–139 for a review of the basic techniques.

All of the joints shown on this page are butt joints—two square-cut pieces joined together by positioning the end of one member against the face or edge of another member. The joints can be fastened with nails or screws only. They will be stronger, however, if you reinforce them with metal reinforcements, dowels, a plywood gusset, or a wood block.

YOU'LL NEED

TIME: About 10 to 20 minutes per joint, depending on complexity.

SKILLS: Making square cuts, drilling, using fasteners.

TOOLS: Square, ruler, pencil, saw, drill, drill bits, hammer, nail set, screwdriver.

Butt joints

Wood block

Corner braces

Plywood gusset

Corrugated fastener with dowels

Flat corner iron

Dowels

Making simple, strong joints *(continued)*

Lap joints are stronger than butt joints and often look better as well. To make an overlap joint, simply lay one of the members on top of the other and nail or screw it in place. For a full-lap joint, cut a notch into one member that is as deep as the second piece is thick. Clamp and glue the two pieces together, adding fasteners if you prefer. The half-lap joint is the strongest joint (see page 143–144).

Dado joints are attractive and strong, but difficult to make.

A stopped dado has the strength of a dado and hides the joinery (see pages 143–144).

For a finished-looking corner, make a miter joint. Cut the pieces at the same angle (usually 45 degrees), then glue the joint and drive finishing nails.

A biscuit joint also is strong and has the advantage of being completely hidden. To make it, however, requires a biscuit joiner (see page 146).

Lap joints

Overlap

Full-lap

Half-lap

Dado joints

Dado

Stopped dado

Miter joint

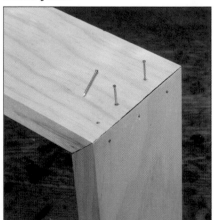

Miter

MAKING A HALF-LAP OR DADO JOINT

Shelves and other wooden structures made with half-lap or dado joints are clearly a cut above those made with butt or even miter joints. Half laps and dadoes are the stuff of cabinetry rather than carpentry. However, these strong joints don't require skills for fine woodworking, just some basic marking, cutting, and chiseling skills. Both joints require precise notches. Use sharp saw blades and chisels. To hone your notching skills, practice on scrap lumber.

Half-lap joints

A half-lap joint is made by removing half the thickness, typically the same thickness for each piece, of the end of each connecting piece. Half laps form strong corners. You can reinforce the joint with fasteners but take care not to split or crack the end. When gluing, keep the joint clamped and allow it time to dry thoroughly. You make a half lap with either a tablesaw or a router with a straight bit.

Dado joints

The term dado refers to the type of joinery and to the groove. The groove is a channel that runs across the grain to a depth of either one-third or one-half the thickness of the board. The connecting board seats in the groove or dado. Make a dado with a router equipped with a straight bit or a tablesaw using a dado blade. Increase the strength with fasteners or glue or both. If you have never made a dado joint, practice a couple times with scraps.

1

MARK FOR A HALF-LAP JOINT...

Overlap the pieces where you want the half-lap joint. You may want to use clamps. Mark for the notch on the first board by running a sharp pencil or a knife along the edge of the board. Mark for the notch on the second board using the same method. Or wait until the first notch has been cut so you can set it over the second board before making your marks.

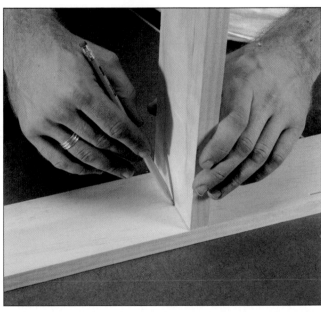

OR FOR A DADO.

Hold the piece that will seat in the dado up against the piece that will be notched. Mark along both sides with a sharp pencil or a knife. Or mark one line and use a scrap piece as a spacer to mark the second line. If you are sure of your skills, use a ruler or tape measure to mark for both sides of the notch.

YOU'LL NEED

TIME: About 1 hour to make two joints.

SKILLS: Precise marking, cutting, chiseling.

TOOLS: Circular, table, or radial-arm saw; square; chisel.

Making a half-lap or dado joint *(continued)*

2 CUT A SERIES OF KERFS...

For a half-lap joint, set your saw blade so it cuts exactly halfway through the board. For a dado joint, set the blade to cut one-third of the way through. Keeping the blade on the inside of the notch at all times, make the two outside cuts, then make a series of cuts about ⅜ inch apart in the area between.

OR CUT OUT A NOTCH.

If your cut falls at the end of the board, simply cut out a notch. Set your power saw to cut a kerf where the notch will end. Taking care to keep the blade square on both sides, use a backsaw to cut into the end of the board until the blade reaches the first kerf.

3 CLEAN OUT AND JOIN.

Using a chisel with its beveled surface down, clean remaining wood out of the notch. Make sure the visible edges are straight and the middle of the notch has no bumps. Dry-fit the pieces to make sure they are tight. Apply carpenter's glue, clamp, and fasten with nails or screws.

DADO JOINTS FOR BOOKSHELVES

■ **Measure twice, notch once.** Dado joints are useful when building fixed shelves in bookcases. Before cutting the grooves, carefully measure where you want to position the shelves. Shelves installed with dado joints can't easily be moved if you want to reposition them later. Also measure the thickness of the shelves before cutting the dadoes.

■ **Check for level.** Before cutting the dadoes, double-check that you have positioned them correctly on the sides of the bookcase so that the shelves will be level when installed.

FASTENING WITH DOWELS

A dowel joint is strong, and you can make one without special tools. Making the joint takes care: You must hold the boards square as you work, you must hold the drill as straight as possible to keep from poking a hole through the edge or side of a board, and the surfaces of joined pieces need to be perfectly flush. Work on a flat surface to keep the face of the boards even. If possible, clamp the boards together before adding the dowels.

Buy a dowel jig if you have many joints to make. Though you can work without one, you will find that it makes the process easier. A dowel jig clamps to the edge of the workpiece and acts as a drill guide. This ensures that the drill bit enters both pieces of wood straight.

HELPFUL TIPS

- Make sure the dowel is 1/8 to 1/4 inch less in length than the combined length of the drilled holes. This compensates for any hole depth errors and eliminates having to drill again.

- Mark the drill bit depth with tape so you know when to stop.

- Coat the dowel with woodworking glue before inserting. The glue adds strength to the joint.

YOU'LL NEED

TIME: 1 hour to make two dowel joints.

SKILLS: Drilling.

TOOLS: Drill with an extra-long bit, backsaw, hammer.

1 TEMPORARILY JOIN AND DRILL.

Position the boards the way you want them and join them temporarily with fasteners or clamps. If you use fasteners, make sure they will not be in the way of the dowels. Square up the corner and drill holes for the dowels.

2 DRIVE THE DOWELS AND TRIM OFF.

Squirt carpenter's glue into the drill holes and insert the dowels. Tap them all the way in and clean away excess glue. Cut off the dowels as flush with the board as possible without scratching the edge. Sand the remainder smooth.

FASTENING WITH A BISCUIT JOINER

Biscuit fasteners—oval-shaped pieces of pressed wood—fit into slots cut by a biscuit joiner. With a biscuit joiner you can join boards edge to edge, join ¾-inch or thicker edging to plywood, or make butt and miter joints.

The key to a strong joint is the precise fit of the biscuit in the slot. A biscuit joiner uses a rigid fence that ensures the connecting slots are cut precisely the same distance from the surface. Coating the biscuit with glue causes it to swell slightly, creating a tight, strong joint.

Be sure you hold the tool with its base perfectly flat against the board as you make the cuts. If you will be using more than three or four biscuits on a joint, work fast and have a helper on hand. Wear hearing protection and safety glasses. Keep hands and loose clothing away from the tool when in operation.

Edge-to-edge joints

Use biscuits when edge-gluing. Biscuits both strengthen a joint and help align the board surfaces. Place glue along the entire edge of the joint to create a strong bond. The boards should be at least ½ inch thick so the biscuits don't create surface bulges. On boards greater than 1 inch thick, you can cut two pockets for extra strength. Lay out the biscuit slots so they won't be exposed.

Corner butt joints

Clamp a support board on the workpiece. Adjust the front fence so it is perpendicular to the surface being prepared. Lay the joiner on the workpiece. Align the indicator mark with your layout line. Use both hands on the tool to keep it steady. Cut the slot.

T-joints

A biscuit joint can take the place of a dado when building fixed shelves. Mark layout lines on the workpiece to show where the matching board will join. Clamp a temporary wood fence on the board. The joiner cuts the slots at the proper offset so the pieces will match up.

1 MARK AND CUT.

Position the boards as you want them joined. For every place you want to install a biscuit, mark a line running across the joint. Set the tool to the correct depth for the size of biscuit you're using. Hold the tool flat against the board as you make each slot.

2 GLUE, JOIN, AND CLAMP.

After dry-fitting the boards with the biscuits in place, apply carpenter's glue to the joint and put some into each slot. Set the biscuits into the slots on one board and slide them into their respective slots on the second board, tapping it into place. Check that the joint is tight, then clamp. Wipe away excess glue and allow to dry.

YOU'LL NEED

TIME: About 30 minutes to make two joints with eight biscuits.

SKILLS: Using power tools, particularly aligning a biscuit joiner and holding it flat.

TOOLS: Biscuit joiner, hammer, clamps, square.

CAUTION

USE BISCUIT JOINER SAFELY

The biscuit joiner blade is safely retracted when not in use. When in use, the blade buries itself in the wood. Still, use caution when operating the tool. Wear hearing protection and safety glasses. Keep hands and loose clothing away from the tool when in operation.

APPLYING LAMINATE

Plastic laminate comes in a variety of colors, patterns, and textures. With practice and the right tools, you can lay down laminate as well, if not as quickly, as a professional installer.

Be sure that the surface to which you are attaching the laminate is straight, smooth, and supported so it will not flex. New particleboard works best, although laminate also can be applied to plywood and old laminate.

YOU'LL NEED

TIME: About half a day to cover a couple of straightforward countertops.

SKILLS: Accurately measuring and cutting, applying cement smoothly, using a router.

TOOLS: Circular saw or carbide-tipped knife; brush, paint roller, or notched trowel; rolling pin; router, file, or sanding block.

<YOU CAN INSTALL LAMINATE TOPS

YOU CAN INSTALL LAMINATE TOPS
Working with laminate is well within the realm of the do-it-yourselfer, unlike more expensive countertop options such as marble or granite, where installation is best left to the pros. Now that laminate is available in myriad finishes and colors, it is an even more attractive option for countertops.

1 CUT THE LAMINATE.

Cut the laminate so it is about ½ inch larger than the surface in both directions; you'll trim it exactly after installing it. Cut it with a circular saw or score its face with a carbide-tipped knife. Cut with the face up if you are using a tablesaw or with the face down if you are using a circular saw.

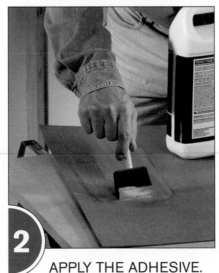

2 APPLY THE ADHESIVE.

Choose professional-grade contact cement, which costs a bit more than the homeowner-type cement. Spread it evenly on the back of the laminate and the base surface using a brush, a paint roller, or a notched trowel. Allow both surfaces to dry completely before adhering.

TOOLS TO USE

■ **Use a router with a special laminate-edging bit.** This will give you smooth, professional-looking edges that you can't get with a sanding block, rasp, or file. Experiment with the router on scrap pieces to set the bit to the correct depth; if it is too deep, you will cut away too much and ruin the project.

■ **For small jobs or for areas the router can't reach,** use a sanding block or a rasp. Work slowly. If you sand away too much laminate, the only way to fix it is to start over.

Applying laminate *(continued)*

3 ATTACH THE LAMINATE.

Cover the surface with brown wrapping paper and lay the laminate on top. (You can also separate the base and laminate with dowels or sticks.) When the laminate is positioned, carefully pull out the paper or supports. Roll the surface from the middle outward with a rolling pin.

4 ATTACH EDGING, AND TRIM.

Attach the edging pieces so they butt tightly against the underside of the laminate piece. To finish the project, trim the overhanging edges of laminate with a router, file, or sanding block. Take care not to crack the laminate or lift it up as you work.

ADHESIVE CHOICES

Contact cement is not the only adhesive for laminates. Many fabricators, especially those working with large surfaces, use polyvinyl acetate glue (PVA). This milky white glue forms a stronger bond than contact cement but lacks the water resistance. Yellow carpenter's glue, an aliphatic resin, is an offshoot of PVA. It works well on small projects such as shelving or backsplashes. Standard carpenter's glue is not moisture-resistant, but some formulations of yellow glue are.

CAUTION

TAKE SAFETY PRECAUTIONS WHEN USING ADHESIVES

Many adhesive products for applying laminate contain volatile organic compounds (VOC). When inhaled, the compounds enter your bloodstream. Temporary exposure to VOCs can cause dizziness, headaches, and nausea. Continued and frequent exposure could lead to debilitating health problems—or worse—over time. This can manifest itself as permanent damage to the nervous system, kidneys, and liver.

Information on toxic elements and how to protect against them is available. Ask the supplier for a Material Safety Data Sheet (MSDS) for the product. This form provides the detailed information on toxicity, correct handling, proper protective gear, and proper disposal of the product. Federal regulations require all suppliers to have these forms available and to provide you with a copy upon request.

Always work in a well-ventilated area when using these products. Use an appropriate mask. Dust masks are useless when it comes to stopping inhalation of VOCs. Respirators with VOC-approved cartridges are effective at filtering out the toxic fumes. Ask your local auto supply store, lumberyard, or home center for the appropriate mask.

SHAPING AND PLANING

Beveling edges and corners, planing doors, trueing edges and ends of lumber—most carpentry projects include at least one of these shaping tasks. The three best types of tools for shaping wood surfaces are planes, surface-forming tools, and rasps or wood files. With practice and a clean, sharp tool, shaping can be a pleasure rather than a chore.

However, even the sharpest tools are no match for a board that's badly twisted, bowed, cupped, or warped (see page 90). Always inspect your material for flaws and select only stock suitable for the job. Don't assume you can shape it up later.

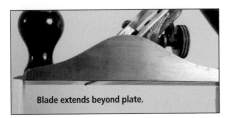

Blade extends beyond plate.

SCRIBING A TRUE LINE

To straighten a piece of lumber or a door, you must first draw the line indicating where the piece should end. This is called a true line. A true line is usually straight, but not always. For instance, a door often must be planed to fit an opening that is not straight. To make a true line, scribe it by holding the piece up against the place into which it must fit. Run your pencil along the opening as you mark the piece for planing.

When scribing a line, check the angle at which you are holding the pencil and the thickness of the pencil line. Hold the pencil at the same angle at all points along your scribe line or you will cut off too little or too much wood. Decide if you want to cut off all of the pencil mark or just up to the mark.

KEEP PLANES IN WORKING ORDER.

Various types and sizes of planes are available. Most carpenters use a smoothing plane or jack plane (shown *above*) and a block plane (see page 150). To help keep the blade sharp, lay the plane on its side when not in use. Retract the blade into the body for storage. If any parts become rusty, clean them with a little oil and fine steel wool. Adjust the blade so it cuts thin shavings easily; you should not have to fight against the wood.

(Labeled diagram: Lever cap, Cap lock, Blade, Cap iron, Tote (handle), Lateral adjusting lever, Front handle, Frog, Body, Depth adjustment knob, Mouth, Toe, Heel)

FOLLOW GENERAL PLANING RULES.

- It takes both hands to operate the tool, so clamp your work.
- Plane with the grain.
- If you get anything but a continuous, even shaving, the blade is dull, adjusted too thick, or going against the grain.
- To avoid nicking corners, apply pressure to the knob of the tool at the beginning of your cut and to its heel at the end of the cut.
- When planing a narrow edge, grip a square-cornered block of wood against the bottom of the plane as you work, as shown *above*.

Shaping and planing *(continued)*

Work straight on for smooth cutting.

SHAPE WITH SURFACE-FORMING TOOLS.

Surface-forming tools come in a variety of sizes and shapes. The one shown *above* works much like a plane. You cannot adjust the depth of the cut, and it will not produce as smooth a cut as a plane, but it is easy to use. You can regulate the cut by the way you position the tool against the material. For rough-cutting, hold the tool at a 45-degree angle to the work as you push it. For a smoother result, hold the tool parallel to the board's edge.

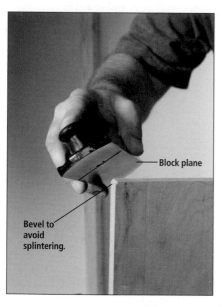

Block plane

Bevel to avoid splintering.

End grain

SHAPE END GRAIN WITH A BLOCK PLANE.

As long as you're shaping wood parallel to the grain, planing will go smoothly. But when you need to shape the end grain, you will be working at a 90-degree angle to the grain. A small block plane works best on end grain. Bevel the corners first, with the bottom of the bevel at the final cut line. Plane end grain from both edges to the center to prevent splintering the edges. On narrow stock, clamp a piece of scrap wood against one edge to support the grain and plane in that direction.

POWER PLANER AND BELT SANDER

If you have a substantial amount of planing to do, buy a power planer. The depth is easy to adjust, and as long as you hold the base flat against the surface, you will get a smooth cut with little effort. Be sure to use carbide-tipped blades or you will have to change them often.

If you work carefully, a belt sander shaves material, especially softwoods, with relative ease. Start with a coarse-grit sandpaper. Hold the sanding belt flat against the surface; you'll make gouges if you tip the tool. Once you have taken off almost as much material as you need to, switch to a smoother paper.

SANDING

Once you've taken the time to cut and assemble your project, don't skimp when it comes to the final steps. Do a thorough job of sanding so the wood will be well-prepared for its finish. Don't expect stain, varnish, or paint to smooth out the surface for you. They will only follow the contours of the wood and often will accentuate, rather than hide, imperfections. Unless you are using a belt sander with a rough abrasive, don't expect sanding to remove more than $\frac{1}{32}$ inch of material; shape or plane instead (see pages 149–150).

USE A BELT SANDER FOR ROUGH WORK.

Use this tool only on rough surfaces and only if you are sure of yourself; it is easy to make gouges if you tip the tool or if you rest it in one spot too long. Always run the sander with the grain, never against it. Don't apply pressure as you work; just let the weight of the sander do the work.

USE A DETAIL SANDER IN TIGHT SPOTS.

For awkward areas, a detail sander can spare you hours of fingertip work. Sanding pads are self-adhesive or have hook-and-loop backing; just lift one off and put on the next one. Work carefully. A detail sander has oscillating action. Because it concentrates on such a small area, it takes off material quickly.

CAUTION

SAND SAFELY

Particularly when sanding with power tools, wear a dust mask. To avoid difficult cleanup later, seal the room.

HAND-SAND WITH A BLOCK.

Except in hard-to-reach areas, never use abrasive sheets alone—always use some sort of sanding block, either purchased or improvised. Sanding with a block is less tiring and produces more uniform results. Tear abrasive sheets to size rather than cut them or you will dull your knife blade quickly. Check that the bottom of your block is clean and smooth. Any debris can tear the paper and mar your work. Sand only in the direction of the wood grain. Sanding across the grain or in a circular motion can leave hard-to-remove scratches. Don't exert much pressure. If you're using the right grade of paper, light strokes are all you'll need.

SAND THREE TIMES

- Take the time and go to the trouble to sand three times, using progressively finer-grit sandpaper. The wood surface may feel smooth after your first and second sandings, but it will get smoother as you move on to finer-grit sandpapers. A common progression is to start with 80-grit paper, then proceed to 120-, 180-, and possibly even 240-grit abrasives. Clean dust from the wood between sandings.
- If you can't sand out a stain or discoloration, apply a small amount of laundry bleach to it. Try several applications until you get the right color. Let dry before sanding again.

Sanding *(continued)*

Wrap sandpaper around wood scrap.

Wind scrap of abrasive around finger.

Roll sandpaper around dowel.

USE INGENUITY FOR TIGHT SPOTS.

When smoothing wood in tight quarters or in unusual situations, special tools can help. Consider buying or renting a detail sander (see page 151) or a contour sanding attachment for your drill. Often, however, you can do the job with a sheet of abrasive and a little ingenuity, as the three examples *above* show.

To sand two surfaces where they meet at an inside corner, wrap a creased sheet of abrasive around a sharp-cornered block. To smooth inside edges of bored holes and small cutouts, wrap abrasive around your finger or a small round object. For sanding outside curves, wrap a sheet of abrasive around a dowel.

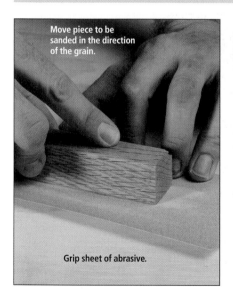

Move piece to be sanded in the direction of the grain.

Grip sheet of abrasive.

Sanding block

Masking tape

SAND A SMALL PIECE.

When you need to smooth the surface of a small item, sand it on a full sheet of abrasive held flat with your free hand. This keeps the surface of the piece even and flat. If the abrasive fills with dust, wipe it with a clean cloth or give it a few slaps against your bench.

ROUND OFF EDGES.

Because wood corners are susceptible to nicking and splintering, it is a good idea to blunt them with a light sanding. Hold the sanding block at an angle; use gentle pressure combined with a rocking motion. A rubber sanding block like the one shown, *above*, is ideal for this purpose because its base gives slightly.

PROTECT EDGES WITH TAPE.

Sometimes you'll want to sand one surface without scratching an adjoining surface. To do this, use masking tape to protect the surface you don't want sanded. Affix the tape carefully, making sure it adheres tightly at all points. Watch closely as you sand and immediately replace any tape that rips or gets damaged.

FILLING AND FINISHING

Paint, stain, and clear finishes rarely cover up imperfections in wood. Often they make things look worse rather than better. It pays to prepare your wood carefully before you add a finish.

Fill in holes with wood filler and sand the surface smooth. If you're applying a clear finish, limit your use of putty to small spots; even putty that is made to accept stain never quite looks like real wood. Even if you're going to paint the surface, cover exposed plywood edges. They soak up paint like a sponge and will look rough no matter how many coats of paint you apply to them.

Once the wood surface is prepared, match your paint, stain, or clear finish to the intended use of your project. See the chart on page 154 for selecting finishes.

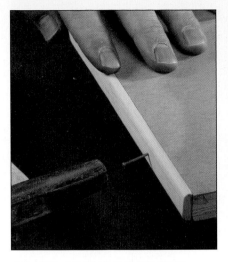

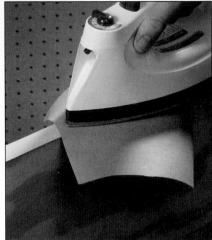

COVER PLYWOOD EDGES.

To conceal a plywood edge, cut a thin piece of molding to fit, apply carpenter's glue to the edge, and fasten the molding with brads (small finishing nails). You also can cover an edge with wood veneer tape. Buy tape that is wider than the thickness of the material and that matches its surface. Cut the tape with scissors, leaving at least ¼ inch extra on all edges. Position iron-on tape carefully, so it covers the edge along the entire length. Apply even, steady pressure with a household iron set on high.

Use contact cement to apply noniron-on veneer. Trim the edges with a sharp knife, then lightly sand the corners.

FILL NAIL AND SCREW HOLES.

For small holes, use a dough-type wood filler. Apply filler either before or after staining; experiment to find out which looks best. Begin by tamping a small amount of the filler into the hole with your thumb. Smooth it with a putty knife. Wipe away the excess with a rag dampened with water or mineral spirits, depending on the type of putty (check manufacturer's directions).

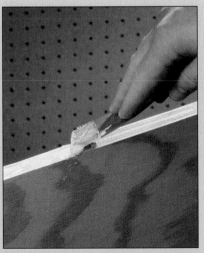

FILL LARGE AREAS.

If you're going to paint the entire surface of a project, water-mix putty excels at filling shallow depressions over a large surface area. The putty sets up quickly, so don't mix more than you can use in 10 minutes. To fill cracks around a knot, mix the putty to a pastelike consistency and force it into all the cracks with a putty knife. Feather out the patch to the surrounding wood. To fill edges of plywood or the end grain of boards, mix the putty to a thinner consistency. Sand and apply a second coat if necessary. For deep holes, you may have to apply two layers to allow for any shrinkage of the first layer of putty.

Filling and finishing *(continued)*

SELECTING CLEAR FINISHES

Adhesive Type	Characteristics	Application and Drying Time
Natural-resin varnish	Resists scratches, scuffs. Spar varnish good outdoors.	Use varnish brush or cheesecloth pad. Dries in 24–36 hours. In humid weather, allow 36 hours.
Polyurethane varnish	Resists marring, durable, remains clear.	Use natural-bristle brush, roller, or spray. Let dry 1–2 hours; 12 hours between coats.
Two-part epoxy varnish	High resistance to scuffs and mars. Ideal for floors.	Use brush. Check directions if coating wood filler. First coat dries in 3 hours; second in 5–8 hours.
Shellac	Easily damaged by water. Clear or pigmented.	Use small brush with chiseled tip. Thin with alcohol or recommended solvent. Dries in about 2 hours.
Lacquer	Fast-drying. Ideal for furniture.	Best sprayed on in many thin coats. Let last coat dry 48–60 hours, then rub with fine steel wool or hard wax.
Resin oil	Soaks into and hardens grain. Resists scratches.	Usually hand-rubbed in 2–3 coats. Needs 8–12 hours to dry.

APPLY PENETRATING STAIN.

Apply stain with a brush and wait for a few minutes. The heavier the application and the longer you wait, the deeper the color. Wipe with a clean rag, taking care to make the color even throughout the piece. To make it darker, apply a second coat. If it is too dark, rub with a cloth moistened with the recommended thinner.

Begin with strokes across the grain.

Finish with long strokes with the grain.

PAINT CORRECTLY FOR A SMOOTH LOOK.

Painting with a brush may seem like a simple task, but here are a few tips to keep in mind. Begin applying paint to wood surfaces with short strokes across the wood grain, laying down paint in both directions. Don't bear down too hard on the bristles.

Finish painting with longer, sweeping strokes in one direction only—this time with the wood grain. Use just the tips of the bristles to smooth out the paint.

ANTIQUING

If you have worn or marred furniture or cabinets, you can avoid all the work of stripping, sanding, and refinishing them by emphasizing imperfections in the wood.

If you are new to this process, buy an antiquing kit, which usually includes base- and finish-coating materials and brushes and applicators. Choose from a variety of finishes: marbleized, distressed, spattered, stippled, crumpled, and others.

Remove dirt and wax from the surface, apply the base coat, and let it dry. After sanding, quickly apply a finish coat. Wipe it to achieve the desired finish. Let dry 48 hours and add a clear, protective finish.

GLOSSARY

For words not listed here, or for more about those that are, refer to the index, pages 157–160.

Actual dimension. True size of a piece of lumber, after milling and drying. See *Nominal dimension*.

Awl. A sharp-pointed tool used for making small starter holes for screws or for scribing lines.

Batt. A section of fiberglass insulation measuring 15 or 23 inches wide by 4 to 8 feet long.

Bevel cut. A cut made at an angle through the thick dimension of a piece of wood.

Biscuit joiner. A mechanized tool used to cut incisions in lumber. Oval-shaped wooden biscuits are inserted into the incisions and glued to reinforce a joint.

Board. A piece of lumber that is less than 2 inches thick and more than 3 inches wide.

Board foot. The standard unit of measurement for wood. One board foot is equal to a piece 12×12×1 inches (nominal size).

Building codes. Community ordinances governing the manner in which a home or other structure may be constructed or modified. Most codes deal primarily with fire and health concerns and have separate sections relating to electrical, plumbing, and structural work.

Butt joint. A joint formed by two pieces of material when fastened end to end, end to face, or end to edge.

Casing. Molding around a door, window, or other opening.

Chamfer. A bevel cut made along the length of a board edge.

Cleat. A length of board attached so as to strengthen or add support to a structure.

Clinch. To hammer the exposed tip of a nail at an angle, bending its point into the surrounding wood for added joint strength.

Coped cut. A profile cut made in the face of a piece of molding that allows for butting it against another piece at an inside corner.

Counterbore. To drive in a screw below the surface of the surrounding wood. The void created is filled later with putty or a wooden plug.

Countersink. To drive in the head of a nail or screw so its top is flush with the surface of the surrounding wood.

Crosscut. To saw a piece of lumber across the grain.

Dado joint. A joint formed when the end of one member fits into a groove cut partway through the face of another member.

Dimensional lumber. A piece of lumber with nominal thickness of 2 inches that is at least 2 inches wide, used for framing.

Dowel. A piece of small-diameter wood rod used to reinforce joints.

Edging. Strips of wood or veneer used to cover the edges of plywood or boards.

End grain. The ends of wood fibers that are exposed at the ends of boards.

Filler. A pastelike compound used to hide surface imperfections in wood. One type, pore filler, levels the surface of wood that has a coarse grain.

Fire blocking. Short horizontal members sometimes nailed between framing studs, usually about halfway up the wall. They serve to slow a fire from moving up the framing space.

Flush. On the same plane as, or level with, a surrounding surface.

Furring. Lightweight strips of wood applied to walls to provide a plumb nailing surface for paneling or drywall.

Grain. The direction of fibers in a piece of wood; also refers to the pattern of the fibers.

Gusset. A piece of wood or plywood nailed or screwed over a joint to give it added strength.

Hardwood. Lumber derived from deciduous trees, such as oaks, maples, and walnuts.

Header. The framing component spanning a door or window opening in a wall. A header supports the weight above it and serves as a nailing surface for the door or window frame.

Inside corner. The point at which two walls form an internal angle, as in the corner of a room.

Jamb. The top and side frames of a door or window opening.

Joists. Horizontal framing members that support a floor and/or ceiling.

Kerf. The void created by the blade of a saw as it cuts through a piece of material.

Lag screw. A screw, usually ¼ inch in diameter or larger, with a hexagonal head that can be screwed in with an adjustable or socket wrench.

Glossary *(continued)*

Lap joint. The joint formed when one member overlaps another.

Ledger. A horizontal strip (typically lumber) used to provide support for the ends or edges of other members.

Level. The condition that exists when a surface is at true horizontal. Also a tool used to determine level.

Linear foot. A term used to refer to the length of a board or piece of molding, in contrast to board foot.

Miter joint. The joint formed when two members meet that have been cut at the same angle, usually 45 degrees.

Molding. A strip of wood, usually small-dimensioned, used to cover exposed edges or as a decoration.

Mortise. A shallow cutout in a board, usually used to recess hardware, such as hinges. Deeper mortises receive tenons to make a joint.

Nominal dimension. The stated size of a piece of lumber, such as a 2×4 or a 1×12. The actual dimension is somewhat smaller.

On-center (OC). A term used to designate the distance from the center of one regularly spaced framing member to the center of the next one.

Outside corners. The point at which two walls form an external angle; the corner you usually can walk around.

Particleboard. Panels made from compressed wood particles and glue.

Pilot hole. A small hole drilled into a wooden member to avoid splitting the wood when driving in a screw or nail.

Plumb. The condition that exists when a member is at true vertical.

Pressure-treated wood. Lumber and sheet goods impregnated with one of several solutions to make the wood more impervious rot.

Rabbet. A step-shaped cut made along the edge of a piece of wood used to join boards tightly.

Rip. To saw lumber or sheet goods parallel to its grain.

Roughing-in. The framing stage of a carpentry project. Framing later is concealed in the finishing stages.

Rout. To shape edges or cut grooves using a router.

Sealer. A protective, usually clear, coating applied to wood or metal.

Setting nails. Driving in the heads of nails slightly below the surface of the wood.

Shim. A thin strip or wedge of wood or other material used to fill a gap between two adjoining components or to help establish level or plumb.

Soffit. Covering attached to the underside of eaves or a staircase.

Softwood. Lumber derived from coniferous trees, such as pines, firs, cedars, or redwoods.

Square. The condition that exists when one surface is at a 90-degree angle to another. Also a tool used to determine square.

Studs. Vertical wood or metal framing members spaced at regular intervals within a wall.

Taper. A gradual and uniform decrease in the width or thickness of a board.

Taping. The process of covering drywall joints with paper tape and joint compound.

Three-four-five method. An way to check corners for square. Measure 3 feet along one side and 4 feet along the other. If the corner is square, the diagonal distance between the two points will equal 5 feet.

Toenail. To drive a nail at an angle to hold together two pieces of material, usually studs in a wall.

Tongue-and-groove joint. A joint made by fitting the projecting tongue on one member into a corresponding groove on the other member.

Top plate. The topmost horizontal element of a stud-frame wall.

Vapor barrier. A waterproof membrane in a floor, wall, or ceiling that blocks the transfer of condensation to the inner surface.

Veneer. A thin layer of wood, often a decorative wood laminated to the surface of a more common wood.

Warp. Any of several lumber defects caused by uneven shrinkage of wood cells.

INDEX

Index *(continued)*

Index (continued)

METRIC CONVERSIONS

U.S. Units to Metric Equivalents			Metric Units to U.S. Equivalents		
To convert from	Multiply by	To Get	To convert from	Multiply by	To Get
Inches	25.4	Millimeters	Millimeters	0.0394	Inches
Inches	2.54	Centimeters	Centimeters	0.3937	Inches
Feet	30.48	Centimeters	Centimeters	0.0328	Feet
Feet	.03048	Meters	Meters	3.2808	Feet
Yards	.9144	Meters	Meters	1.0936	Yards
Square inches	6.4516	Square centimeters	Square centimeters	0.1550	Square inches
Square feet	0.0929	Square meters	Square meters	10.764	Square feet
Cubic inches	16.387	Cubic centimeters	Cubic centimeters	0.0610	Cubic inches
Cubic feet	0.0283	Cubic meters	Cubic meters	35.315	Cubic feet
Cubic feet	28.316	Liters	Liters	0.0353	Cubic feet

To convert from degrees Fahrenheit (F) to degrees Celsius (C), first subtract 32, then mulitply by ⅝.

To convert from degrees Celsius to degrees Fahrenheit, multiply by ⅝, then add 32.